# MIDWINTER CONSTELLATION

written on December 22, 2018

Stephanie Anderson

Hanna Andrews

Julia Bloch

Susan Briante

Lee Ann Brown

Laynie Browne

Shanna Compton

Mel Coyle

Marisa Crawford

Vanessa Jimenez Gabb

Arielle Greenberg

Jenny Gropp

Stefania Heim

MC Hyland

erica kaufman

Becca Klaver

Caolan Madden

Pattie McCarthy

Monica McClure

Jenn Marie Nunes

Danielle Pafunda

Maryam Ivette Parhizkar

Khadijah Queen

Linda Russo

Katie Jean Shinkle

Evie Shockley

Sara Jane Stoner

Dawn Sueoka

Bronwen Tate

Catherine Wagner

Elisabeth Workman

Mia You

# MIDWINTER CONSTELLATION

Black Lawrence Press

 Black Lawrence Press

www.blacklawrence.com

Executive Editor: Diane Goettel
Book and cover design: Shanna Compton

Published 2022 by Black Lawrence Press.

Printed in the United States.

in their lives
penguins set one day aside to catch balloons

so don't forget to send them some

—BERNADETTE MAYER
on *Midwinter Constellation*
November 2021

# CONTENTS

# ACKNOWLEDGMENTS

PORTIONS OF THIS BOOK were written on the ancestral homelands of the Nimíipuu (the Nez Perce Tribe) and the Pelúuc (Palouse) Band of Indians; in Cheyenne, Arapaho and Ute Territory; on the land of the Wahpekute, of the Očhéthi Šakówiŋ Seven Council Fires; in Mohican and Haudenosaunee Territory; on the land of the Penobscot Nation, part of the Wabanaki Confederacy; on the ancestral homelands of the Coast Salish Peoples, the Lummi Nation and the Nooksack Tribe; on Lenapehoking, the unceded territory of the Lenape; on the illegally occupied land of the Native Hawaiian people; on the land of the Confederated Tribes of Grand Ronde; on the land of the Cayuga and Seneca Nations; on the traditional, ancestral, and unceded territory of the Musqueam people; on the lands of the Munsee Lenape and Canarsie; on the occupied homeland of the Wampanoag and Narragansett peoples; in Kaskaskia Territory; on the traditional lands of the Shawnee and Myaamia peoples; and on the unceded lands of the Eastern Shoshone, Kickapoo, Iowa, Sauk and Meskwaki, Tohono O'odum, and Pasqui Yaqui peoples.

We acknowledge the presence of native people since time immemorial in these places we are privileged to call home; we honor ongoing tribal ties to these lands; and we are grateful for the sharing of traditional ecological knowledge.

# DREAMS

If I could train my dreams it might be
only to be able to remember them.
If dreams might be the impressions left
from yesterday mine would be of lions,
3000 years old, shot with arrows
along a cold expanse of stone, or
the favorite pub of Marx and Engels,
wrapped around with Christmas lights.
Or a golden helmet buried inside a boat
turned into a hill, some trees, the wonder
at who might look at a hill and see it undone,
dug and sifted away, like my daughter
now wiggling out of her blankets,
waking to yet another day
in an unfamiliar city.

Prelude to Dream:


We can trace the I Love You words written in your book
With translucent paper, shake the snowglobe containing
Only snow in front of the white and red candle at 1:11 am
On Midwinter Day's eve nearing the Long Night Moon

Seconds ticking down out of this world yet time can stand
Still in a Zone late at night the longest night of the century
Yet morning comes early and bright with the city fog dripping
        Over the veiled buildings


                White string lights suspended in a neighbor's
        Window one street over—I will probably never know them


Another bank of windows in front of that—drapes drawn
Diaphanous moon where are you? Full up there maybe I
Can see you—Yes! Straight over head—the clouds pass


                In front of you   O moon     interrupted or praised by
        loony laughter from someone walking down 22nd Street


People are wet but not too cold tonight—soon it will be
        "Punishing" again as it does get that way up North but
Today is temperate—actually *too* warm—
        I've been inside
All day except to go to the roof
        and I called Bernadette around 8:15pm
To wish her Happy Solstice and when I told her I had been
Cleaning cleaning so that someday I could finally write a poem
And she says she does not clean anymore—it just makes things more cluttered
        Which I now believe is true
                        I've got to quietly move the papers
And boxes I dumped in order to make myself sort and not wake my snoring
        Husband and get to sleep so I can wake up and get on the bus
    To go read all of *Midwinter Day* aloud with others in person and
        on the ether waves

I start to get the late night stillness effect and begin to see
   All of these strange things which began to surface from my cleaning
Like an advent calendar with its original
   Red envelope which need only be opened 3 more days till Xmas

   What presents I do buy I usually lose and then find later
      And eventually get them to their rightful owners
      Why is it that I have so many objects swirling around me?
The Letter M on a monogram in a catalogue—
   Was it chosen because it's in the middle of the alphabet?
or because it stands for monogram?   I love all the Letters!
         I've got a branding iron from my great-grandfather's ranch
      That says "V.D." for Van Dunlop—   how's that for branding?

         I wonder who of the other poets writing this poem are AWAKE
   Like me   and it's already Dawn in Amsterdam!

   One more time to go see the moon
She's moved further over
         Can't see her from my window
      And now to Dream

+

Only image

   •

Only action I can hold onto
   Is the necessity of pulling root vegetables
Up from ground and storing for winter

Parsnips, carrots, stored again in sand to be replanted in spring—maybe it's what my great-great grandmother whose name was America had to do in Montana or maybe it's related to those strange turnip-like beings I saw floating in the pool a few months ago and I pulled one out and wrapped it in a blanket like an ugly humanoid subconscious thought that needs to be swaddled and fed and taken everywhere like an adult-sized baby.

Jennifer who is skilled in dream-combing observed that I often dream about getting things for free like when I ducked through the line into the movie theater and I first thought this was a bad thing like a moral judgment as when CD laughed at me for taking a roll or two of toilet paper from the Crab House restaurant in Providence when I was a poor grad student, then I thought of my early obsession with the *Borrowers* and how they made a life from "borrowed" objects like a cigarbox with a fan for a headboard for Arrietty's bed and a spool for a table but then I think of how so much of what I write is "borrowed" from the words around me beaming in to start or write the poems

+

I've been remembering my dreams in technicolor detail and writing them up or down till about 2 weeks ago and then they have kinda submerged but somehow give further energy to the mind of day

Silas Rose has been sleep-talking throughout the night,
now rolled off the mattress onto the hallway floor.
He sleeps in a closet meant to house a washer and dryer
our temporary year. Can the year itself be temporary?

Yes, it can. I dreamed I wasn't doing well, but there
was pleasure in seeing a stage full of children dressed
in Native American cottons like the ones Cathy showed
in her slides. I recognize them as midwestern, particularly
the red bead-bib tops. Bruno sleeps, their father sleeps too, landed
at one in the morning. Bruno will have nightmares and Silas
will have had nightmares because most of what humans have
is nightmares. Their father won't remember his nightmare. I swing
a little virtuous rising early, but there's a flood of work to correct
me. A machine hums, chewing mold out of the small atmosphere
of my bedroom, an expensive and subtle iron lung. No. A real
iron lung would probably have cost a great deal more. I took
my pill when I fell off the bed, actually, says Silas and he has.
Every morning I must check to see if the children have taken
their pills. They don't grow larger without them. We turn on
the pinkish lights of the artificial tree and the star-shaped lights
wrapped about the real wreath and a lamp on the table we bought
in the woods for $25 from people who'd won the lottery.
Silas illustrates a card for a multiplayer game he says takes place in a demon
     realm.
Hearing about someone else's multiplayer game is the same as hearing about
someone else's dream. That is, it's easier to get interested if it's well told
and I like to hear I've appeared in either, which often I have.

*The root of desire is intimacy;*
*the root of intimacy, desire.*

                    paradox leaves its residue
                    upon waking

koan or catch-22
how do they feed each other
how do we?

I dreamt I was on a bike ride down curvy country roads with my ex-husband. He was being followed, but somehow I wasn't. I was pointing out all the good hiding places up ahead—how about that barn among the sheep, etc. He wouldn't get off the road, the bicycle. Was he a wolf among sheep or a victim among men? Was I trying to keep him safe or trying to get rid of him? Why don't men seize opportunities to save themselves along the way? Who am I to believe in salvation?

The sun is not yet up over the trees.

I can't emerge from dreams and record them because there are no dreams, there is no sleep, there is no Google doc; I cut myself off, I guess, from my imagination, my friends, the collective. There's only the baby, who is old enough that I should be sleeping, but who only sleeps at my breast; there's my sick husband, my sick mother; there's the drive through the night, my resentments, just give me an hour, thirty minutes, do you want me to throw you out the window, I hate you, the Christmas tree glowing its solstice, your consolation is this light in darkness, this proof that life is beautiful at its cruelest, fucking Yule is your dreaming now

3:03 I dreamed something, for a minute. End the year at the house where you grow up

6:08 dreams of villains and fiscal responsibility; Marilyn killed Lily (her avatar/old self?) through debt

Stuffed dates three ways; missing the marathon, parties. Baby slept so well (for 4 hours) that the bed is a lake of milk (IRL)

6:31 girls in tits out???
(later: what did this mean? Prediction of my morning: they were?)

Ring ring and rain. I open my mouth to speak, hollow in a Midwestern way. I say to you, *for someone who had a gay brother die of AIDS I'd think you would treat queer people better.* I say to you, *you know I'm gay, right?* You say "That's reductive." I am going to hit you with my fist of fingers turned flowers. I am confusion. What is reducing? Divisible? The dream is hazy from here. The morning's reactions are stars. A telephone somewhere, longish cord, the heft of as I wrap around my body full. Merry Almost Christmas. In the dark and a phantom limb singing cordoned off wire. If a rib cracks midrun, will anyone in miles see me fall? The big dog is in the poop yard howling for the little dog to come home and the little dog is dead, put to rest the day after the election, a bad omen. Ring ring. How to face the shortest day with the longest dread.

       I woke myself dreaming this poem,
some lines about a tiny table with a heap of words on it
and the ache in my jaw I get sometimes
when I grind my teeth so hard I cracked one
and had to go to Dr. Sheth to get a crown

                Now I'm finally
the queen I'm meant to be I joked, but it's 4:34 am

& I wonder if you're up too, dreaming this poem.
I've woken Shawn who brings me a glass of water, who I want
to tell about the earlier dream involving the pink squares
I rearranged on the screen

      but I reach over for the eucalyptus oil,
drop some on my wrist so I can breathe it while I sleep.
Eucalyptus is dusty gray, with those little round leaves. All
the notifications on my phone are about a partial
government shutdown, midnight's glass slipper, &
Katy sent an email about some hashtags.

        Later I'll give some
to the poem if it seems like a good idea. In *What's Your Idea*
*of a Good Time*, Bernadette writes to Bill with whom I once
discussed the spelling of Maybelline as in eyeshadow she writes
about her dentist too, a man who wears a gun! She quit seeing
him saying she prefers being "worked on" by a woman

i wake to dreams draining from my brain, down the circuit of my spine,
and into my gut, where some kind of acid will turn them into instincts i
can't explain. emotional residue today says i was content or curious in the
rooms my subconscious built for me last night—there's none of that after-
nightmare panic, and none of the desperate longing to return to whatever
situation was salving an ache. time for waking dreams, the ones that have to
squirm out from under my superego's ass.

In gray light I can return to the house in the dream
of Nino Nanette, the cyclist who has lost their peloton

and we have become their surrogate. The French woman
down the street is hosting us but we are very far away
from Powderhorn. The table is wide and we have to invent
the present because the circumstances keep flickering
in the dream but also necessarily in this twilight recall.
As if insistent on staying there, the future will not brighten.

                            Each iteration has its own aura
and governance like Frank Big Bear's portrait of the Patti Smith's
we passed on the way to artifacts from the sunken city—
each dream here its own cargo—ergo—lost world.

                                      Nino
is fatless and laconic—a dream rendition of our intimacy
its lack or a cris de tour—to move past static interpretations and Nino
is no oligarch or pugilist and Nino is no snowman or debutante
in the nationless morning of the 3rd government shutdown
in two years and Nino is the naked intensity of anarchic refusal
      next to the page beginning I am exhausted.
            I wake up at 4 something to B at my side
of the bed asking to join us yes of course this is the party and I don't wake
  again
until gray light, E saying something I can no longer recall
of practical import and me finding myself
with my hands on my head as if I am standing in a windstorm
       and my hat will otherwise blow away. Hey nonny, nonny, crack
your tired cheeks. Belbinus said the book beside me says that Mares
when they smell the smoke of a lamp put out
bring forth their birth before it be perfect.

One long bookshelf, just higher than my head
stretched along a wall of windows looking out onto forest

Whereby my mother turns 65 and takes all yall's crowns I tweet in the
dream after going to the yard she in white hair high makeup where there
were eyes pink is for the insides fear there too no more meds I cooked
something while she stood there looking hot someone said I think that's
it all there was nothing about my mother nothing about misha nothing
about bridges of madison county i watched for the first time before bed
love and how we found each other once nothing about eternal recurrence
I read before bed and when from the dream came her words Morning. Ur
boy had a good nite while I was down there, till c1215 on my chest he likes
to sit, lol and when I move he doesn't go nuts, lolol . . . . . . . . Another pack
came . . . . . so what time u go to Jeff and Jasmine??? Staying till tomorrow???
My boy my cat peter who is crazy just like she both of them sequestered
in her basement like memory while their meds get right peter who i let
walk on her lawn i see what kind of mother you're going to make she said
another pack package a gift for misha's mother whose 65 birthday (she is
the one turning 65 my mother has been there) we will be celebrating in kiev
on nye a sky blue planner personalized in gold from bake studios i like that
name flown in from australia where i've never been for her to track the most
beauty yet jeff and jas bought a lakehouse in put valley and yes i'll be staying
there until tomorrow I don't text back

I cannot remember but I woke with a headache. Does it count if I speak
about asking for dreams the night before? I lit familial candles aloud
surrounding bloom of amaryllis. I woke at 2:42 am and replied to a text

from my sister. Yes, I'm ok. But what did I dream? Dear Bernadette, I'm so ready for Midwinter Day for the light to come back. I stood there calling to the light. Come back! Come back! Luminous light encircling and becoming being. Please do not elude. Dream and calm into presence. Like a steaming bath. I must have dreamt of a mikvah. I've never been in life but I did in dream separate myself from this past year in this way. Is this a dream or is this a body of water? Does it matter? I am immersing. Dear blessed water or dream or light, I love you. Please stay in the stately arms of the embrace of all of our children and ancestors, friends, sisters, loves, remembrance of we.

On the third morning, the linen has become familiar against my cheek. I wake to a creek or a rush I don't know, a sound that fades almost instantly, that hazy no-place—not home & not here. The dream place? Am I always dreaming of another location, of locating myself finally in technicolor, some unmappable surround?

What shoes does one wear to cross the river?

Why do I wake most mornings with only a question—usually mundane. A question & an understanding—that the dreams were long & intricate & it was hard work getting through them. Every morning, waking with new, unreachable knowledge. I feel this heavy today. There was an orange light & there was travel & many voices. My daughter's. Many others. I try, as I always do, to scroll for the dream image, anything that translates better than the truce of having been *elsewhere*.

But the only thing remaining is the question of shoes & water. & the body, which has gone a great distance.

Last night we listened to Joni Mitchell after dinner, cleaning the kitchen & then after that, while everyone else drank wine & I watched the snow fall in giant flakes—the kind that in Brooklyn usually meant a short, but gorgeous, flurry. Now I wake with her, too, as if she was a witness to the dream—I am traveling, traveling, traveling . . .

I am not home.

In the basement room, the paperlike blinds are backlit. Greylight. Aya shifts on the air bed. The room is filled with sleep breathing, in tandem.

My dreams are tiny, discrete, mostly untroubled—one marching after another like clouds or mice: My grandmother expertly summarizing family complaints, me choosing fillings for buns—chicken or crispy duck? There are words I scrawled through half-sleep—"dented," "morose"—having spent the week practicing dreaming and eating foods for the encouragement of dreams. Two garbage trucks begin emptying dumpsters, and Genevieve turns on the news. We drink coffee together in the dark.

I was leaving class my class at the university. I was taking myself to eat alone at a bad Italian restaurant. There were no windows. There were no seats. I was going to sit underground, and the food was bad.

Why was I alone? Where were my friends?

And then I remembered I could leave. I walked out and around. Sometimes it is hard to begin something new because it takes time. Habit and efficiency keep us in awful routines. I walked out and through buildings without knowing my destination. I found a market. I bought some fruit. I went back to my dorm room.

Packages for my daughter were going to be sent back undelivered until someone in the mail room saw my last name and thought I must be her father and thought to send them to me. Even in my dreams I am enraged at the patriarchy. My daughter opens small, blue foil packages of cloud. One says "cumulus." My cousin is in my room. Or my cousin and I share a room. She has boxes of what I think are Italian pastries from home. Even in my dreams I am inspired by food. But there's nothing in the boxes but cheap imitations.

I leave. I am leaving Austin. I am in my car. I am trying to get back on the highway that I know well, that will take me where I want to go, but I get confused at an exchange. It is not the highway I know. It is one on which I might have to pay a toll. But I keep driving on it anyway. The sign on the side of the road marks the first mile as 0.

You sleeping lightly next to me in little puffs of breath, Ishi and Elsie on my legs, tumbled together, I got drunk last night on sake, not too regrettably, and that's how I went into the puff of dream, you were there with me, we were very small in a vast experiment of human life, bumbles and worries, bad decisions wrecking the planet, we were trying to decide how to take responsibility, to be open and incautious too, and earnest, but realizing how cruel it was to be put here as an experiment when what we wanted was to respond truly and unmeasured to circumstance. I tried to explain that within the experiment other experiments were necessary, smaller ones we could live inside to be alive to our living. Of all our friends Pamela understood this and also that though life is repetitive we are able to experience every day differently. She made me promise to travel to Seattle to see the nurse log kept in a room and that one needs an appointment to see. I asked if it was a dead log, she said yes, but living too. We promised not to be killed by academia. We promised to render our service to dream, art & poetry. We promised above all to be kind to ourselves, that would be our experiment. You dreamt of pumpkin pies floating down a river, they tasted good. My sister dreamt of being squeezed through the birth canal. She said it was memory. My brother dreamt of building too many houses. My brothers dreamt of being more fluid. I was told a protein is not alive and this confused me. A friend said you can't do bad science and call it poetry. I have to agree but wonder why poetry isn't science. With smoky hair I did not dream of fire.

I wake up in the afternoon, still in my dream, so angry I could spit. I punch Jake in the arm and say, "I'm mad at you. You accepted a blowjob from a woman named Julian who was a YouTube makeup artist working at the beachside hotel where we were also doing some kind of seasonal work in exchange for room and board. You possibly got a blowjob from her friend, too—a woman in her seventies wearing a Pilgrim style collar like Ruth Bader Ginsburg. I'm also mad that every room had a theme and ours was 'numbers.' I hate numbers. The room next to us was themed 'Lolita.' I would have liked to have that room. But the orgies I tried to join in it were dull; no one made me feel truly wanted. And when small children needed to travel home from the hotel, we had to strap them to big seabirds and act like we believed they'd make it safely. And when I wanted to go for a run on the beach you wouldn't come with me. You wanted to sit in the sun with our beautiful neighbor with good brows. Even my friend who'd cried on my shoulder the night before left me on the boardwalk after promising he'd go with me. And when I went to the cocktail hour I was introduced to a horrible professor as a potential man to have a fling with that night. It was insulting. Then I was talked into taking a selfie with a girl who I know dislikes me intensely. And the Marionette lines on my face were deepened by the cheap red light. When I stormed out of the resort after the blowjob incident (of which I had no proof at all; it was just a feeling in the room) and got on the bus out of there, I changed my mind just as we hit an arid border town. I thought 'I'm glad Jake isn't here; this place would scare him' and just as I thought that, a truckload of men with rifles and glocks jumped out and ran into the bar shooting, then out again, shooting. The man they were shooting jumped up on a fence in front of me. I realized I was not as hardened as I have thought myself to be for many years without question. And the girl with me was very large, which prevented us from both fitting on the floorboard as the bullets ricocheted off the windows. Eventually, I made it out of the crossfire and back to the hotel. But I was still so mad. I drank the vodka in my room with cranberry juice and coke, but it wasn't enough. I wanted to drink with other people. The bar wouldn't serve me; they said to go drink whatever was in my room. A kind of therapeutic sharing session started up on the pool deck. People talked about friends they'd met during summers spent at the resort who'd been lost to drugs or had disappeared because of the criminal lives they'd led. The owner stood up and read an early story by David Sedaris, which he'd published in his first zine when they were roommates at the hotel in the summer of '75. It was a bad story, and I'm just so pissed I had to listen to the whole thing when I could have been awake with you."

Jake is on his laptop changing our flights, drinking coffee made from beans that were digested and pooped out by squirrels for the enzymes, as I tell him this. The radio is tuned to NPR; David Sedaris is reading a story about a character called Santa Freud. Jake asks, "What's your middle name?" I say, "That's it; I'm leaving," and get back in bed.

I look for something to hold and remember first only my sister
eating chipotle peppers out of the can at our dinner table in Houston
and a politician's mouth swallowing the screen through which
he speaks. Dreamwork is a synthesis I try to master, if mastery is even
what I want. Yes and no. I struggle with something I know, wake up
anxiously looking for what fell out. I could drift back into David's breath
and keep that part of him in the world I left, look for the other people
who might also be there with me. My sister who dreams of me
watching her eat the peppers at the dining room table. The man
whose guilt-ridden face came from a screen, who sees me seeing
himself consume that thing he so desired to eat. I remember now
my mother in the dark talking to me with no face only her knees
showing in the dark under the down pink blanket in flowers talking
about the plot her brother left behind. That was all a real thing.
What isn't a real thing. There it is, coming around again. Somebody
somewhere gives me a name I think I know but something, what,
does not sync.

In dreams my body still wanted
water, the new blinds are
drawn, I knew; this is the bed
I've always wanted and Laura is
still here beside me, my mouth
is dry and the bedstand glass
of water too warm to drink,
warm as in the same

temperature as my body
and there weren't many dreams I remember
I think because the night was full
and late with Kurt Vile changing
his guitar for a banjo and a new flannel shirt
at the same time he almost
never stopped playing
but part of that was the trick
of so many lights like casino bingo
in this new ending world of competing
attention machines, not
the bingo I knew as a child,
pressing colorful plastic chips
to letters with my own small fingers
and whether winning or losing, afterward balancing
the chips on the sheet and carrying them
carefully across the classroom
to dump them in a bin and then move on
to an arithmetic lesson now so much
a part of me I don't recall exactly
what I learned and still do
and this I know is the dream

I don't dream but wake at 5.00
thinking about work I wake
up when E goes to the bathroom
& A says I don't dream but mommy
wake up      I say          put on the coffee

I grab the clock
of the mother's elbow
in the dark Georgia square
she asks
is it wet where I come from
is it ever warm
if I wake up at this time
will I make it by that time
have you seen my bundle
I insist
you were supposed to watch it
or I was supposed to watch it
either way there was some
kind of watching
Actually
it's too early for dreams
too dark for watching
only with the skin

It's a dream road and I recognize it from other dreams suspended impossibly from a place I know but don't. A sliver that twists windingly jagged above water. The ear is full. The car with people I know but don't the water glints dangerously. It is a dream about getting someplace, a frustrated terrible self-conscious desire. Stuck like a record. Who is with me? I move for my glasses and it all slips inevitable seeing as glass flying through the open car bottom into some abyss of course. After the fight's hot tears and the long delayed love I slept harder more desperate dreamt less

I say I'm scared of getting close to people, getting hurt
(In the dream this seems an original thing to say)
She says oh let me show you
She has trouble lighting the match while she's driving
It breaks partway and frays at the top
The flame blazes over the broken bit
She says to put it in my mouth and close my mouth
Which I do and feel no pain, the lack of oxygen extinguishing it instantly
I see what you mean, I say

Weird how you're supposed to be okay on your own. Matt wakes me up at
8 says he's going surfing. I think it's the work week but it's Saturday, the first
day of our winter break. I don't remember my dreams just him scared in his
sleep, and rubbing his chest in the night until his breath went calmer

★

I wake up in the winter dark in my parents' house
this room was my sister's not mine
she's a nurse now, working nights
          and does her dreaming in the day
her little dog curled beside her          I read
until I hear the children coming, still dark,
my husband smooths a hand along my body
but it's a mom-body now
               morning is here
daughter's smooth cheek          a bundle of clothes

she's brought to change into
left by my lamp as she runs
to find grandma

I wake when you wake you
keep waking I'd been in a
karaoke bar where everyone
was moaning or was that

                    days ago?
You wake again your face
cold I carry
          you to the white bed
whimpering we wake you are
a younger *baobao*
            head to board
and then rotating like
an hour
       hand the wind wants
inside, and again I wake
in blue-white winter light
like stone outside and heavy.

                  ★

this morning i laid in bed as m. slept and tried not to check work email.
i found myself reading or rather googling articles about genesis breyer
p-orridge. i'm not sure how they came to the front of my mind. i want to
train myself to remember dreams by practicing in advance but i forget. last

night i remember falling asleep before midnight and then slept through the night which is unusual lately. i wake up often, afraid i might crush the 10lb. dog, a fear i've had since m. mentioned it months ago. i'm no longer alone enough but often lonely. i think about the project of physically joining two bodies—the pandrogyne—the becoming plural. my ear aches.

In the dream we're moving in with Maxe and Diana, no we're moving next door, no it's a duplex where someone gets the downstairs with the fireplace and someone gets the upstairs with the electric stove, no both have fireplaces, and it turns out it's been a room attached to our house all along we just didn't know it, and we didn't know all this time that if you look out the back wall of the house it's a beautiful view of trees and water it's New Zealand. Maxe and Diana are out so Emma helps us unpack and puts stuffed animals everywhere which don't belong to us we don't know where they came from they're eyeless and kind of frothy. And the stove is electric and I have to get back to writing the poem about stereocilia for Patrick and desire is a kind of exit.

Liminal spaces, and then here we are. Slowly into the gray of night and day. Today you were there, and then not again. In my deepening eyes something past me, and even still, past that, to the tops of trees where you live now. Good morning, deep into the day, and we are here anyway. How even in dreams we hold each other closely. In the waking, who is there? Am I alone? I place my hand on the heart next to mine, the weight sinks further until it disappears.

The truth is I am lionhearted. Dreaming
no match for the waking flame. We fell asleep smelling smoke,
placed damp towels on all the sills. Now the ground is frozen
and in the dream, distance evaporates. I say every word
held back, bold in touch too, lengthening in spirit. The mountains
shadow the rust of the cold day breaking and we hum with energy. Winter
keeps us lucky, rested, like suns.

Are you pressing me forward in this dream, ghost
of life in every one I want to love? The hallways
branch in the pressing dream, a bluster and a patter
beyond my sleep (a sus between the teeth around
the esses and the tees), beyond the needy ghost my witch
friend sensed bumbling around me, and I do not know what
behinds me anymore, my desire, now all this aforeing.
Death to nuclear supremacist good. When you picked me up
from Wassaic, our talk immediate and deep, abouting
Venns (velvet of the nose at opening), my temples glowed,
periphery of woods abstracted. Here was a beautiful pie,
you dream, an aperitif you wanted, sweet and smoky.
We passed the forge house in the Shaker Village
on our way to the ritual and we imagined me
pushed around the great space, sweating voices.
I learn Yule logs involve a mean kind of discipline,
soil dives, and wishes because I free myself to change
the metaphor like Bernadette with just a quarter
(nickel?) of sound.

# MORNING

In the earliest-lit northeastern corner of shitstorm America,
something maybe about a stick shift and something about gainful
    employment,
I don't remember now: the complicated dreams of the overtired,
interrupted by my lover's morning erection—the one I recently called
*like a kitchen counter, a slab,*—cuddle-stabbing insistently
as I am the border wall fallacy between his lust and
the baby, now nine and a half, under the covers on the other side
for his morning routine, more habit than need,
*but which is the migrant?* Trick question: none of us. All of us.

The dogs cross over all of us with their elastic bodies,
rolling onto their backs and moaning, their paws skyward, and I say that
    they are singing
Teddy Pendergrass's *Having a Christmas Party, ever-ree-boday.*
They must be let out. We all must be let out
from under the brown flannel and grey flannel.
There is a flood watch. There is an ulcer developing
inside my lower lip so I am going to apply the bee pollen tincture
which is the only thing I've ever found that works
and it works like magic (or actually like tincture).
You should try it. If we still have bees next year.

There is a partial government shutdown.
There was a malignant tumor in Ruth Bader Ginsburg's left lung

(*full moon in Cancer today,* Lee Ann reports).

There is a cropped oversized modal-blend tank top we got at the All
    Saints outlet

still wrapped in white tissue, perched like a nest

on top of my dresser, which I can see from my bed:

it is charcoal-colored with two large tigers curling their tails fiercely.

Everything I want right now has tigers or leopards or studs or women

shouting.

Eleven years ago yesterday we buried

our second baby in the pine woods overlooking the Penobscot—

Bernadette, too, knows the pine cones.

We have not gone to visit that little slate disk in the loam in a long time,

and may tomorrow. It may make the children cry.

I will almost certainly cry at that little redhead we lay in a tiny wooden box

and how we had to leave him wrapped in Buddhist white silk alone in the
    forest

on that coldest snowiest darkest day, after which we ate muffins.

If I rise then I have to vacuum up the dog hair from the stairs,

scrub the mascara off the bathroom counter, plan the holiday meals.

This is the first poem I've written in a long time and I don't want to stop
    just yet,

but I should go get the bee tincture and the cleaning spray.

Jane squiggles into my brother's childhood bedroom (Paul is quarantined
in mine). "Is Alice awake?" Baby is blessedly sleeping. "I'm gonna go
under," sleeps at foot of the bed. Sky is gray, trees are an old copper color

that only seems to happen in RI. Jane climbs up: "tomorrow's Christmas Eve! Why not?"

7:59. I'm alone with these children and no one will help me.

The google doc link begins to feel like the free babysitting I thought I'd get from my mother, the standard help I would get from my partner. The cavalry isn't coming. The rescuing ship receding into the distance. It's just us. "Did you see what Alice did? She slid my snot right out of my nose." "She grabbed on my pajamas . . . twice . . . and she . . . hit my pajamas . . . a lot . . . she's doing it now." both my & Jane's real-time litany of complaints.

Paul can't touch the children because he's recovering from a stomach bug. My mother can't touch the children because she's taking a medicine that suppresses her immune system. I will never get to take a shower.

Becca sent me the link and it's still early in the morning and I'm here, in this white text box, in this wide white bed. They're cuddling and vocalizing. I have basically only yelled at Jane despite her enthusiasm for Christmas & her sister, things I hoped to encourage. As soon as we get up we need to wash potential viruses off the sheets. Hand sanitizer is useless, the Internet said. I'd still like you to use it, my mom said. Terrified she will get this. I could have stayed in NYC, gone to the marathon reading, gone caroling, but touched no one, of course, moved among my fellow travelers like the ghost I am right now

Again I have ruined a nice morning by trying to document it / trying to keep too much of it for myself / under this lace coverlet

It's morning on #MidwinterDay & this is how the river looks,
with New Hope beaming under a dark sky. I'm not awake enough
to write yet, nor asleep enough for the hypnogogic state
to bring much magic. The coffee is already gone & we have
forgotten to turn on the miniature tree.
                                        Across the river there's someone
who erects a wooden A-frame, and covers it with lights, which
can only be a thought for those of us across the river, across
the border since no one else can see. If I get up early enough
it's still on, throwing colored lights on the water which this year
has not frozen yet because it's overly warm for December.
Living on a river and a border between states I'm constantly
looking across means I can't help but think of the newly erected steel
slates so pointedly lethal. I guess I mean hypnopompic
though, that zone we creep through after sleep
on the mornings we don't snap open like a newsfeed.

Emerging from the tunnel beside Katy
    On the full big blue bus
Past the guy with rainbow mohawk
And little nubs implanted in his forehead
    To attach the horns we course up New Jersey
Winter highway—only color is the light blue sky


Hashtag no makeup / Patchouli is the scent for Midwinter Day


A trip to the Glitter factory     What is Glazed Glitter?
    All glitter is impossible to remove

Vapors and ingots of the visible spectrum drawn to shiny things
    Like foraging for honey and licking plates with shiny surfaces
An invention so recent it's barely defined
    An intangible type of sparkly light
Foil cut into tiny slivers    it was simply everywhere
    Silhouettes—the first is in New Jersey and the second is in
New Jersey—Glitterex
    He would not allow me to hear glitter being made
The Glitter Factory: I agreed to not describe the building's glorious
    purpose
According to the New York Times read aloud by Katy
Colonized by Pixies    floor of crushed moonbeams
    Arranged by color formulations and size
Forklift flecked by tiny scarlets
    Over 1000 jumbo jars of
What appeared to be samples of the Nightsky
    collected over the Atlantic Ocean
The prettiest shade was slightly violet
The biggest seller is always Silver
    The sparkle of twitter glitter as glazed as Cliterture

To be put on things that do not have glitter on them
    As in the rainbow Glitterbombing of Newt Gingrich by Nick Espinosa
So useful for politics
    There is nothing intrinsically rainbow-colored about the glitter itself

        (Hawk Sighting out bus window with cream-colored breast!)

Various luminous colors with different reflective indexes
    How many layers is multi?

Each layer is half the wavelength of light
Imperceptible by touch

I have a jar of magenta glitter given to me as a gift
    that never seems to deplete no matter how much I use it

Glitter takes about 1000 years to degrade
    The bad news is that means it's in the ocean
Anything we do is now called glitter

Blue violet plantain red clover tea from brooklyn herborium for stress
bumps on the chin before i wash my hair

I have fed everyone breakfast and arranged for children and me to be dressed
to go to see A Christmas Carol. My mother dressed Jane after I screamed
and screamed at Jane for waking the baby. I have never screamed so much at
a child. I think the stomach bug is starting to get me.

I'm angry it's not easy like: we'll just have bread. Feed everyone
bread and cheese and myself with wholesome achievability.
That's not the 21st c. It's dopey out here where bodies can't digest
comforts turned toxic. Bernadette asks then why do we husband
this food? Well, why do we. Still. Forty years later. Everything
is a gut compromise. I game the bone of a large animal

so that I might get more done. Greg makes a joke about
Post Modern O's and Reagan sends a phrase from a 19th c
Icelandic lullaby that reads *sleep, you black-eyed pig / fall into*
*a deep pit of ghosts.* Today a day is as though we live a family,
but it's a holiday in that it's unusual and no one knows
what we will live a year from now. Coffee spikes. I write
a student a long note that's easy to write because she writes lovely
things and they're not yet done, nor are they too vexed, I need
only ask her next step and enjoy the last, that's alright. Coffee
spikes and I know I could use it to get one or two more done maybe
I don't use it often enough to love my children. They dress themselves
if you ask them to. They have pursuits. The littlest shows his father
a trick with cups, his delight plain as his taste for sweets. I don't know
that I delight in anything I should. I should delight this morning in the fog
that hovers slow over silver grass and the pinkish light, how one can sit
somewhere soft to work even if work is hard.

pack a suitcase, pack a poem. portmanteau. what
can be folded. what can be doubled up. what can
be rolled into one. gather a few recyclable pieces.
what you can arrange and rearrange :: layers. a
strong statement piece that'll take you anywhere
in any weather. this is a poem :: we're flying
economy. we pay extra for anything that won't
fit.

Evaporating like leaves with certain music coffee insists blue penetrates white and branches and every desk flowers from unknowing. My fingers speak with something like linen or apologetic fumbling forward falling back into my own hands. Two teens are sleeping nearby still in the location of dreaming, growing into their own beings. Developmentally what is a person in the middle of winter moving directly into this exact moment? We do not hesitate. I used to know a word whose name was morning. I once had a friend, a reddish flower. We walked or worried or woke up into the next hour. Come with me. Along the banks of every whispered aspiration for a day. Not ahead of ourselves not above or below the moment but inside the feathery sight of now.

I used to know a word
        whose name was myself. This self
would wake late, take half hour showers,
        wear delicate fabrics, emerge into the world
only when ready. For a long time I didn't mind
        I gave her up, but lately glimpses of her
come back, she feels within reach, but only
        in the comedy of saying, "I have to go
to the bathroom," and that small voice, "I need to go too,"
        and then waiting in the small, hot space
of another's urgency and demanded accompaniment,
        and in the tragedy of never ordering
what you want to eat because you're counting on
        what everyone else is eating and what'll be left,
so you get half a pancake, cooled,
        with two-and-a-half slices bacon, worse cooled,

and remember you're on vacation!

and everyone just wants you to have a good time!

but first can you tell them where
        the toy tiger is and of course they have to brush
their teeth while you shower, the hotel room
        only has one bathroom, and besides
"I just have to tell you one thing . . ."

The alarm goes off, but I am the only one to hear it. Still mostly dark, even here, this close to the bottom of the night, at the edge of the country, false edge. I turn on the radio, listen to today's disasters: "Most mornings I would be more or less insane" writes Rukeyser. Farid wants to sleep more. Gianna doesn't move. In the back rooms Patti and Ariane, Farid's cousins visiting from Paris, are awake because their bodies feel the day before ours. Patti showers. I make coffee but the milk is gone. Do we need more? If I pour myself over Farid like a blanket, in bed, buenos dias, bon jour. Gianna now up and Ariane and her pantomime across languages with the Christmas presents we let them open yesterday. I pour bowls of Cheerios, make more coffee. Nothing gets done before the second cup, Patty says. I pull towels from the linen closet. Pour water. Send Farid to get milk. Gianna listens to the Deathly Hallows audiobook. She's heard the story a million times, but tells me the voices are like her friends. Friends in language. Friends in vowel and moan. The heat through the vents sounds like ghosts, my mind, more ghosts in my family this midwinter than ever before. Less family? It feels that way. Blood thins. Or "Your blood has thinned" is what my family used to say when one could not suffer the cold, but in my family suffering was a virtue.

Coco cries at the top of the stairs having found me
missing. I come up to bring her down and the now
midsleep practically ritualized trip to the bathroom
the interval event which seems to eat all dreams
turns into a meeting with the dog who must sit making
body-to-body contact and the new kitty who moves between the sink
and the Christmas cactus precariously placed on the edge
of the tub by the block glass windows wet in blue light and
the pile of dirty clothes so significant in front of the radiator
it becomes an animal too.

In this meeting of everything more supernatural than otherwise
we decide to stay awake.

          Forecast as depicted: 7am cloud 8am cloud
9am cloud 10am cloud 11am cloud. My feelings read like vapor too
unlike B who suddenly with us is mock annoyed at being awoken.
Coffee oxymel water the green friends spin 18 times in front of the
morning committee fast. Good morning, high pockets. Cold O's with
milk for the famished, one of whom is already costumed. Crystal Palace
vs. Manchester City—the green of the pitch otherworldly. Overdue:
Verlaine, Nadja, and Yeats's catalog of human encounters
with faeries and the mountains and woods having their day, their day.

Aya climbs in bed between us, her morning ritual. At home she says
"Can I cuddle?" But here, in mystery light, in another time zone
says: "When is it going to be wake-up time?" She kisses my nose & the air

around my forehead. She sees me writing & says: "Why are you doing this?"
"I'm just writing things that happen—things that I am doing on a mid-
winter day" I mumble, sleepy-mouthed. "You're so cute," she says.

I want to wash my hair & daydream of a long shower with the honey lemon
soap in my in-laws' guest shower. & coffee in one of the small cream-colored
ceramic cups, which somehow makes the coffee taste better.

+

Good morning, screen glare. I'm working again because the University
can't figure out its funding & I'm administrating & editing on top of my
full-time job. Logged feedback & grades for over 200 essays in the past
2 weeks, but no break yet—I'm combing HTML forums for good code
(varied column widths in WordPress) while my family eats huevos
rancheros upstairs. But Eryn brings down the coffee & it is just how
I like it.

+

Upstairs not a single light on in the house, but sun floods through
whole walls of glass, double beamed off 6 inches of snow on the
preserve. I miss monochrome Chicago winters through the small
studio window—gray lake, gray sky, the piles of graying snow
flattened filthy with bus tire tracks. I miss Northeast mornings,
cloudless sky white & holding, wood stove smoke charring the
air outside. Here, yesterday, the narrow streets crowded with
holiday skiers, the lifts cycling back & forth like an amusement
park ride. I'm thinking now at Aya's delight in seeing her breath
in front of her.

★

coming out into morning breath
blown in my direction David greets
& talks about the cats who are so quiet.
I know they listen for a change &
something comes. There it is. Balki cries
at the door & David gets up. I still try
to remember what I lost, catch
a goose honk and a train in motion
plane sounds I thought as a kid
were clouds were in transit. I read
about the shutdown, steel slats
& think about how there is a nation
who funds in droves architectures
manifest of fear & want for a place
that makes—what. Their own sideways
Tower of Babel. Something to be closer
to—what—

How do you strike when the thing becomes lateral—

I look at other people's pictures, Daisy
sharing a picture within a picture. Iris watching
Men in Tights. I go back to sleep
for a minute. it's not what I want
take me to what I left—

I can't go back. Callous as steel
slats. There is a testament I

have held like salt so long
on my mind. I remember
a comic book bible my mother
bought me & pictures of
the tower coming down
& the story of Samson that does
not fit the other: the story of
a boy they try to humiliate
& the faces of the boys
on his side who only see
victory & the face of a blonde
who shears on behalf of face
I don't yet see.

(Why don't I get out of bed)

I listen as David
opens the bathroom door
listen as both cats cry
David locks them both
in the office
opens a can
opens the door
& out they rush
I don't go back
don't get up & watch
the clouds, try
to catch birds
in my window, watch
& try to catch them

& say to
who knows:
"tonight will be
the longest night
of the year."

We didn't intend to harness technology to lie in bed longer noticing the day brightening with this kitten now purring on my chest, but the experiment is forgiving. The skylight is rimmed with crystalline ice and in the cold beyond bare branches of the walnut tree, the one limb limp where it snapped in a summer storm. The tea kettle is empty; the sink it is full. There is much I don't remember but there is much not worth remembering and there is what I will remember today remembering as Bernadette remembers. This part is sponsored by kittens. This part is sponsored by government shutdown. This part is sponsored by friendship. This part is sponsored by screw your wall. This part is sponsored by the tree nursery that was last century.

We look out and see the solstice fire still smoldering, a trail of smoke rising from the center of the charred log. The magpies in the maples chirr and chatter, the grass a pale yellow under morning frost. I think about last night and its lessons, the importance of gathering, not what was said or what one remembers, but the importance of love. We make our coffees, old hands at this, your french press, my drip cone. At 9:48 a.m. welcome the Full Cold Moon.

You just need to go into the day believing that, whatever that task, you are there, despite how it blurs you.

I hear you in the kitchen, a quiet cough, another, dishes, I cook eggs, and toast, egg yolk yellow orange juice and a text from Pamela: prepare for mud and bring your favorite plant shears.

Three dried apricots. Fleshy baby feet. My brother has asked his girlfriend to be engaged to him. With my MeMaw's old ring. But I thought I'd lost the ring in high school? Every week for 16 years I've felt guilty about that at least once. Who will make me a treasure. The ring doesn't fit her ring finger, so she curled it over her pinky knuckle. I'm going for a run. Maybe I'm cursed. Now there's only twenty minutes till my appointment. I'm not going on a run. I'm not eating. I'm not going to make it to my appointment on time.

Milwaukee, Abraham
asleep in the poet's room
of our new home
and Laura asleep too
so I am the only one awake; I left
the dream imagining a sunbeam,
just its light, and very clearly,
without emotion, only wanting
to imagine light, and hinge
to a day as gray as I expected
when my eyes and telephone woke
meeting in light some might call false
but in its generation I feel

truths and know moments later
from the weather app that outside
there's a cold the same temperature as my age
and Abe's gone through the front door,
scoots as he says to his grandmother's
one hundred and first birthday party; how
could you even write 101st and believe
age, I can't and am, I don't think I'll make it
there, and how delighted I was to learn
she still kicks his ass in cribbage every time
and I asked him if cribbage was her music,
as in most people age and forget
certain things, decorum or names, the location
of objects or their bodies,
but typically not music; the songs stay even
after the mind has emptied all but the scores
coming out of the mouth as notes,
and yes, Abe said, cribbage
for her was like that, and there's a cake
the size of a car trunk waiting
with her name on it for the party,
and when he left the door swung back open
to let in the warmer light from the hall
and Laura said the cats are going out too
so she rose and closed it
and did not come back to bed.

No light today, sweet sun divided, sweet sun pulls back nutrients, impatient
for spring such a touch of better mornings await me. How can I even know

what's there? Between thick sludge coffee and too sparkling of windows—
how chrysalis is what I crawl back to.

★

Fluffy eggs in pink ceramic pan

Being far away from everyone you love
        starts as personal novelty
        ends as cultural condition

Past the fog-erased farms of Iowa

Paint on the red brick of Dubuque
        announcing faded family businesses—
          surnames shared
        by my high school classmates

Crossing the Mississippi should feel so majestic

Instead it's smokestacks and train cars
        at a standstill
It's nothing like New York Bay
        and why should it be

Industry a purpose
        beyond grandeur or shortcuts

I put on "Mississippi" to hear the line about
crossing the river for love

but I'd forgotten the part about
        how you can come back
        but not all the way

which rings out, blessing and curse,
        as we enter Wisconsin

Did I choose to drive first
        so I could control the music
        (our new rule)
or so I could let the poem build up inside me
        like a song

Driving and listening to music is writing

        just as for Bernadette
        tape-recording and taking
        pictures and making
        spaghetti and dancing
        to the Talking Heads
        was writing

Our only conversation so far is about places
where it feels possible to live

which is our only conversation

Impossible to conclude
        without knowing the future

so we keep returning to it
      and sometimes to these towns

Do I need more than one intersection to survive

Do I need sidewalks to thrive?

Street life a luxury too poignant to consider

Curving through the Driftless

Ice hanging from the rocks highways got sliced into

Sides of the road blanketed with seed

Like the best of our solstice intentions

I change all the linens in the house & clean
the bathroom in order to avoid The Poems.

The day coalesces into distinct shadows and patches of light. I catalog
objects returned to the museum: kimono, nautilus, crucifix. Ann says her
father, who built a career in fluid dynamics for aerospace, began studying
medicine in his 50s. Movement is easier to see, she explained, in viscous
fluids like honey or blood.

Are we there yet?
I just want to get to NY
and leave the midwest horizon flatlining

I *want* you, mamma. I want to read a long book. I need
help don't
help me. Arms legs tangled all over
the bed. Such pleasure so close to someone
screaming. Mamma she is touching me. A hug
for everybody. Michela is packing
clothes and sorting
her jewels. Pia uncharacteristically
focused stacking magnetic blocks.
No one will eat breakfast. Make
a smoothie with suspicious juice and fruit. *Ramona Forever* again and again
child hair swooping over book. Pia
wants a book like her sister. Could I eat
breakfast, mom? This is not my breakfast.
Pia uncharacteristically
slow to rage. Maybe
for the peace in the house. That thing
I can't get out of my mind, what Gwendolyn
Brooks said, about children
and a peaceful house. Peter
sharpening knives to bring
to the house where is family is even now
beginning to gather.

cat paws my lip with one claw bared
doesn't hurt me just wants me to know
her guttural trill, she's off the bed
I-75 traffic    neurons firing silver hiss?
or noise diffusing in two ornate and balconied
skin rooms my head turns louder

10am already thinking about death.
iPhone autocorrects "death" to "Edward."
I imagine myself in the future saying, I had a full life with him,
and now I don't want to live without him.
But I imagine myself saying it to my mom, she'll be gone too

★

Morning and it's not cold in Portland, not compared to Vermont. A
sweatshirt is enough for driving with my mother to walk circles in opposite
directions past the manicured lawns of Garthwick, which are flat enough not
to wind her, so we drive there, even though it always feels strange to drive
somewhere just to walk there. As we get out of the car, she says "your sister
won't walk ahead of me even though I tell her to go ahead. Rita always says
'the second child wants to be with.'" I don't think it's a guilt trip. "You're the
oldest, so you're independent," she adds.

I run a bit and try to call Hannah, but she's packing probably, getting ready
for an afternoon flight out of Boston, so I call Bridget and we walk and

talk fast about assignments for our spring classes. I tell her how folklore is defined by its transmission, person to person, changing as it goes. She's interested in information literacy and the rant some Medievalist wrote on his blog and wants to ask her students to dig around and talk about it.

Mom and I walk in opposite directions, so we give little nods or flutters of the fingers as we pass one another and pass again.

I've forgotten the book forgotten
morning's form so I pick one, decide
on a time to leave the room with
its empty white drawers, climb
upstairs to see your faces, small
one cackling with glee every time
the cat stalks by, can I eat this cheese
while pregnant, one bathroom
breakdown later you are reaching
for a gold sphere and I see all our
faces, yours reflected in the photo,
mine wide with the depletion
of love where I think I've come
up short to find even more rooms.

overslept by two hours as did m. and it was harder than usual to get up. m. said yesterday was the solstice and i disagreed because today is midwinter but it's unclear to me if that equals solstice or not. i know there's full moon and meteor shower but i'm not sure i know what that means either. i don't make coffee, just gather myself and go home to regroup and then go to albany but first a bit of guilt for sleeping in. it's warmer outside than expected and i'm not sure what to wear or how to wear it or whether the weather in albany will be the same as red hook, mid-40s the kind of warm that says perhaps a chance of snow.

i want to try to avoid the internet until at least 2pm.

is the process of writing at various times of day and writing in a way that is just writing akin to automatic writing? i know once i type this i will want to edit and revise. i will want to change details of the day into fiction, rather myth, i will want to shape my self so that i can look in a different way.

Desire is a kind of exit, when I open the notebook I see notes from one of the last midterm election phonebanks, tracking the calls: checkmark Thomas, checkmark Kathleen, checkmark Joanna, checkmark Suzanne, checkmark Amber, the software automates the calls feeding each number but leftover from the landline GOTV days of my youth I still fear calling someone accidentally twice. Morning is more thinking about stereocilia and Mairead's lines "The book is not written for you / You don't have to be friends with anyone in it" and half decaf is the new regimen which does help with the sleeping but I always have two cups and trying to figure out what Huebert means by "nontelic grammar." Last month I went with my father to Russian class and Portuguese class at the community center. In Russian there is one word for potato and another word for mashed potato: purée, and "'soup' is soup." "Who remembers please?" We watched the video for "Shot of Vodka on the Table" and my dad snickered and then the Portuguese teacher taught us the line "The wind is crying." In the poem about stereocilia I'm trying to write about echolalia but I don't really understand the edges.

S. delivers her vegetables
and we learn
Bernadette's braids are gone.

# NOONTIME

From Shoreditch High Street take the 149 bus to Fenchurch Street. It's a double-decker bus like in the postcards and for sale at the Lego store. Buy a hairbrush at Boots and wish the cashier Merry Christmas. From Monument take the Underground to South Kensington. Think: "Where fishmen lounge at noon: where the walls / Of Magnus Martyr hold / Inexplicable splendor of Ionian white and gold." Think about how horrible the British press is about Meghan Markle and love that there's an American named Meghan being a duchess here. At South Kensington follow the signs to "Museums." Follow the group of Chinese tourists who also look bewildered, who also have their children in tow. The tunnel is long. Take the next turn to "Way Out." It's better to walk above ground. Enjoy the sun is shining, it's too warm for a scarf, it hasn't rained on you yet.

For Noontime I'd planned to take a walk around town
but I don't feel like it yet, & there's soup to heat & miso
to whisk into it & our coughing to soothe. Ewok texts me as I'm
writing this that our tribute reading for Joyce Mansour has been
accepted for a festival in spring, in a city I love & where it is warm
& noisy in the way I like. O I feel delight, Danielle, when I think of you
& them & your Narnia surroundings & all the years we have written poems
into the same pockets, our trinkets collecting along a long
shelf I keep in my head & how I said when first meeting you

I liked your necklace it was a bird & you said oh birds
kinda creep me out & I instantly felt your delight

Shawn makes a thumping
as he walks through the hallway, the downstairs clinic
is closed for several days so we can play records in the middle room
& has deposited a cup of tea because he is always bringing me
something to drink & who can help but put that into the poem
since it's supposed to hold us all & everything

If I were feeling better & less quiet I
would put on real clothes & shoes & walk into town
& not write about soup & tea & playing records
but this is the real everyday today. Don't feel obligated to
write me back, but Bernadette was interviewing Bill & asked him
*What are all the nouns that you would at present call yourself?*

I make blueberry pancakes for lunch "with a shot of seltzer"—
which is really SodaStream—& try to get the kids to leave the house
for an "art hive" at the nearby museum that is a repurposed schoolhouse
complete still with white porcelain water fountains that smell like pencil
shavings

so we can *make something* instead of just *consuming*
but I am surrounded by Cancers (full moon in) who find their shell
so cozy
& Tauruses who don't want to budge & as much as I too want to be home
to bake miso-tahina cookies & look at the reprints of 60s Japanese
photography magazines,
I am Scorpio & must propel constantly forward lest I choke.

(I am trying on these ampersands I borrowed from Shanna's closet. // They look cute on you, xo S)

noontime: gray
cat, blue
socks, silver
laptop, red
yogurt, purple
coffee mug,
bronze bust,
green shower
mat, white
tiles, black
locks infiltrated
by gray.

Why did I think rage could live in my heart next to my love for the children with no cross contamination / What is the incubation period for ancestral rage? Like five years. I wondered at my own patience, how it never happened, never came out at them, the historical hairbrush/holler/knife. It happened and it was ecstatic, it felt so good to scare someone so much, transfer my fear into a tiny body. Symptoms appeared today, December 22, 2018. Incubation began when. My grandfather's death in 1967 or so. Whatever tanning of whatever hide. My mom came and rescued her from my screaming, which was ironic, but also how grandparents work—they rescue you from the monsters they made.

In the car alone with Jane I said "that was scary, I'm sorry, parents shouldn't scare kids." An apologizing parent. But also don't wake the fucking baby, Jane. We listened to "Sister Winter." We went to the play.

O wait lunch! We forgot to have lunch. We ate caramel corn in the theater and I had a Fezziwig Punch, which is champagne and cranberry juice in a plastic cup. I got some for my brother and then told him the stomach flu narrative, how I watched it spread through my friends on the Internet until it got to Paul. My brother pointed out that the epilogue of the story is him getting the stomach flu from this Fezziwig Punch. I haven't told him Alice and I slept in the bed that his family is supposed to sleep in. Marley descends extravagantly from the ceiling. There is red and green confetti. These are the carols that, in 1989 and 1990 and 1991 and 1992, made my Christmas joy. It incubates and erupts at different intensities. Some inoculation, some vulnerability. When I see the back stairs in the theater where the racks of costumes hang, and the mirror where I stared at my beautiful red chapped lips and contemplated my mortality. When I see these Boomer actors who were Bob Cratchit age when I was Little Fan age. My dad picking me up from rehearsal and taking me to look at Christmas windows the night Papa died. Jane laughs at Scrooge's delight at his own pants. In the lobby Jane shakes Scrooge's hand.

We'll go out walking at noontime it's suddenly mild a day of rain
and the snow melts off a day of rain and soft things wake in the gutter
pretty New England town across the pretty New England river no one
mention that this landscape has a deadly way its pines pitch into its sea
but instead let's go in search of a great big candy cane a special one
large and unique at Ampersand and let's go in search of a coffee let's go

in search of a thing we can't feel most days because while every day contains
everything, it's not particularly easy to pull one thread to the surface
without the bramble of others. I'm always pulling the golden thread.
When I was young and I lived in New York, I met Marie and I went
one night to a De La Soul concert in her company but we didn't really
talk. Posdnuos had a baby that night. His wife did. They didn't go on
until 2, they played till 4. Bruno had a panic attack at the library
and we haven't been back since. He owes a book. It's overdue and
and I think there shouldn't be fines for children too big for mothers
to keep track of their books their books go in their rooms and they don't
ask you to read to them. You ask them to read to you. Read to me, I ask Silas
and he reads me *Lost and Found* it's a book about a penguin lost at land
and the boy who crosses the sea to return him to the South Pole, but no
that's not what the penguin wanted, he wanted only a friend and his friend's
stories, me too penguin, me too, let's paddle through the long year.

noontime is an hour
full of disagreements
like good coffee spilled
into the kitchen sink

Dio runs into each room we clean
each one a vexation

what do you do
when flesh and blood
care is unreciprocated?

we take up the problem
& think about how to move
the furniture

everybody wants something

I tell Dio you can't always
get what you want then pull him
from the closet shelf

Blackstone Castle Company
The House on the Rock
The Cave of the Mounds
NoATC(.com)
Dreamy 280 Cattle Co. Farm Store
Grumpy Troll Brewery
(Caution: Tractor Crossing)
Mt. Horeb Trollway
Mt. Horeb FFA Toy Show
Fisher King Winery
Johnson Creek Premium Outlets
Hunting for Land?
Frank Lloyd Wright Trail
BoostProfits.net
Kettle Moraine State Forest Southern Unit
Fleet Farm (Farm & Fleet?)
St. John's Northwestern Military Academy (hello, ghosts)
Ten Chimneys Nat'l Historic Monument

Luminary Walk & Live Nativity
Buck Rub Archery
Party With a Pig! Pig Roasts
Pettit Nat'l Ice Center
Milwaukee Mile Speedway

at noontime on 22 December 1978 I was
7 years old in Exton Pennsylvania at the corner of
Woodview & Longwood    there was a big
tree at the corner & all the neighborhood
kids would climb it & have what
they called 'a rumble'    it was on
this corner that the nextdoor neighbor boys
beat my brother Jim up one morning waiting
for the schoolbus    their mother
held their bookbags so one boy could hold
my brother's arms behind his back while
the other boy punched him in the face

Russo's for $100 worth of provisions on the way upstate.

My family is freaking out about Christmas and I suddenly hate it like I
hate the sound of ice under pressure, the sound of chewing. Then Alice
comes in with photos of clay food and the day becomes possible again. How

noontime goes is this: oil lamp, candelabra, bust of Napoleon, porcelain figure (some gorgeous youth whose hand, holding a rose, keeps snapping off at the wrist).

I am writing morning in the poem, the moments while living inside the poem, or with the poem as so many layers surrounding me in the world, and this reminds me of nests—not the ones I may one day build, but the cup of them, and what they hold. I wear the smell of the fire into our afternoon and this makes me think *I feel fucked*, thoroughly taken with it, taken it in to me, and the night into me, and the moon that arced across the sky, first appearing over the giant fir trees, then a dot and quite full and high. Later Pamela will tell me that she's a fiery person, and that fiery is good, when you know how to handle it.

The world is straight ice here too
Pretty as an empty mirror
Wind off the frozen water
The pet walk rough white
Your hair in your lip gloss
Apple sore
The ice lake keeping all the fish

I'm driving to meet Julia and Rachel. First time to see their house just a few blocks away from A-Space where the marathon will happen. When I arrive

Julia is lighting candles, Rachel is in the shower. Meadow is asleep with one eye. We are drinking tea with mullein and I remember making mullein tapers dipped in tallow, plucked from meadows, but not meadows of cats. We walk out into the cold air like neuroplasticity. The poets all electric and we've never, any of us, been exactly in this room together on the solstice.

—*Here's the pita bread.*
—*Peter Pan*
—*Aquí tengo pan dulce*
—*Dicen "pan arabe" en español*

We pass cheese and salami, pita bread and panettone from the front to the back seat. The car drives past the Catholic Charities and Islamic Center, out to the edge of our city, into the nthropocene, making the anthropocene, our car and something more in three languages and three continents of legacy, but I don't want to get too sentimental here.

Before we left the house Gianna sat beside me on my office couch to say I miss Grandpa. And I know he's here, she says pointing up, but what I miss is talking to him. I know, I say, I imagine what he would say often. But she says we can't hear him.

I don't believe in heaven, don't talk about it to her, when she asked me years ago what happens after we die, I showed her a leaf, pointed to a tree. Like the leaf, falls, and dies and turns in the soil, to feed a flower. A fumbled around some notion of change and cycle—all dirt, all ash, all star. But how can particle and dust compete with angels and clouds.

Some ideas speed past our intentions like box cars seen from the highway, like the song her French cousin sings in the back seat: *Feliz navidad, propsero año y felicidad. I want to wish you a Merry Christmas.*

Cars and cars and poorly timed shopping. Filling a house near our house with everyone's particular staples. Not raspberry preserves, we need blueberry jam. At least three lights before we can turn. Keeanga-Yamahtta Taylor and Naomi Klein on a podcast talking about the border, the Green New Deal.

Day at halfway point in time also in space
A pirouette turning toward hill for privacy
Performed by tree I'm passing in a car

Am I the only one on the elliptical listening to a Spotify playlist called all the number one hits of 2018 and I'm hearing them all for the first time. I like the song where she says, "I wanna f*ck but I'm brokenhearted, I wanna cry but I like to party." Dave used to tell me I was confused when I went out partying as a form of mourning, and I mourned the last call and I mourned the bar closing and I mourned driving home and getting into bed. He said you confuse staying out late with having fun, what a ridiculous thing to say. I confused my breakup with a good time I confused having a body with being alive. Then there was a dance cover of Fast Car by Tracy Chapman, which was ridiculous but also so good.

"Do you want a birdy in a nest?" mom asks
but I want to shower first and get the cold sweat off, she doesn't sweat herself
just takes a shower and then goes out for her constitutional
"I don't have much in the way of secretions now that I'm 73" she tells me
I come back from the shower and find it's avocado toast and an egg instead
but now the children are hungry too so I make them quesadillas
before I eat anything, heat up the string beans, zucchini,
and still kind of crunchy vidalia onions in the microwave
they both want lots of sour cream, Vesper is coughing
not blowing her nose, snot running a bit down her lip
but clear at least

We are given little tins of tea, try to show you the sleeping cat but you can't
see it for itself when it's curled like a comma, and in the *DiDi* you drop
off or out like an unfolding sheet, Look, he still sleeps on you I say.

The light never really lifts. Actual perpetual dusk
just as our melancholic weatherman warned us. Really
Minnesotans probably revert to talk about the weather
as a quietly desperate way of normalizing
                        its gothic potential for horror—hoary and
doomish
            or not
                    we take off

our costumes—C does I mean—the handmedown velveteen gown
and crown gets replaced with a long sweater vest over her pajamas
                                    (which I never know
how to say so I say it both ways—puhJAMahs, piJAHmahs—a real
Double Gemini, Sag sun solution—how are you feeling? Miraculous
*and* horrid)—the vest produces an unintentional
elfish effect. Sorry, little wolf. A thin dusting of snow
that had fallen in the night has blown away from the rooftops
like puffs of smoke it is cold—and we have bundled ourselves
and are trundling up the alley towards Powderhorn Park,
a jaunty and loudish expedition, complete with Finn the pugilist
leading us north. Powderhorn is named for the shape its lake
once made that resembled the bullhorns shooters of guns filled
with gunpowder, and probably named by the colonial terrorizers
as the name first appeared in an 1839 survey of the Fort Snelling
Military Reservation & terrorists they were as at one point their strategy
for occupying unceded land was to expel all indigenous people
from the state, offering another possibility into the dominance
of weather in everyday discourse, as a way of avoiding
the dark history of how this got to be, this mess. If you google it
*Minni* is the Sioux word for water and *Sota* is something like mist
but *Sioux* is French for snake so wouldn't a more accurate attribution say
the name of the state derives from Lakota/Nakota/Dakota. What
do I know except that even our etymologies conceal & carry. *Smoke*
*& mirrors* is American for history. Powderhorn, the neighborhood,
a kind of island in a larger terrain of segregation. It especially
felt like an island the morning after the 2016 election when
grown-ups were weeping at the bus stops in front
of their children. Powderhorn Lake also has an island itself—one
that is home to cormorants and herons, ducks, geese, and egrets—once

someone even spotted a coyote on the island when it was rumored
to be visiting the neighborhood, which E and I can confirm.
One night that summer we were out smoking on the porch and heard
first creature nails on the sidewalk then the coyote stopped
in the gap between the lilacs to regard us

I have an appointment for a deep tissue massage, which I've
been looking forward to for months. I used to get massages
regularly before I had a child. It's been about 2, maybe 3 years now.
Aya is sitting on the tall metal chair at the kitchen island, writing a poem.
She writes "The world is a whirl." My father-in-law is half-watching
MSNBC & a panel of experts is critiquing the last panel of experts &
I hate that the 24-hour news cycle is background noise on a morning
where the ice glitters in the sun & my daughter thinks about herself in
relation to the universe.

On the front landing, after saying goodbyes, we wonder about
her restless body in the tall chairs—we go back in the house to
set her up on the floor instead. Unnecessary but a small consolation
for me; I can't stand being apart from her. "I'm crazy close to you" she
reminds me, my mirror fire sign. I know it's good for her to have time
with her grandparents. E & I hold hands—a united front—& walk
outside again. It is colder than yesterday & I can smell his face salve,
spicy warm against the freezing air.

E sweeps the windshield with Aya's ski glove & tries to run the wipers
but they're frozen. We drive fast to keep up with traffic down Parley's
Canyon toward Salt Lake, listening to *Scorpion*. It's a stunning & dramatic

drive along the Wasatch mountains, but as we descend into the beehive
the inversion spreads over the skyline. I love the New Wave synth
of "Summer Games" & turn it up. Eryn says he wishes Drake & The
    Weeknd
would make an album together but I think the emo-Drake ship has sailed—
so I love this track tucked away on the B side. It feels like when E & I first
    met,
taking long, winding car trips through the Colorado mountains, with *Take*
*Care*, then *The xx*, then Destroyer's *Kaputt* on the radio.

Breakin' my heart—Breakin' my heart
Break-break-break-break-break-break-break-break

drive slow on route 23 truck honks as i exit take the turn that goes to 87
which i think is also the new york thruway but i don't know. the movie
theater in kingston seems to have closed. I don't worry about surgery
only the possible expenses associated with it and the incomprehensibility
my insurance company prides itself on. driving I wonder where my body
recovers best. dread the drive home.

At the exact full moon in the Albany Train Station parking lot
Katy bibliomanced "sweet" and then a dream that turns to ash

From the middle of *Midwinter Day*—We get a text from Marie
Saying when are you guys getting here B wants to start

I walk in and meet Veer for the first time 6 months old soft and tiny and
strong blue eyes like Alyssa and round, round head she grabs my finger

Just now on the way to say hello and hug Soph and Zola playing cards in
the front of the cafe

I saw a drawing of a bee going up in an atomic bomb on the front of the
New York Times Magazine

Bernadette's genius of the poem is unfolding how she can be
So lyric like a grand Eclipse or actual Solstice
Cosmic skein or stein forbidden remembering
But she remembers moment to moment passing alive
Like rhyming "weather" and "after"
*to you I turn to sing     on the eve of a festival*

We are here together at last in the Hudson Coffee House on Quail Street

Is it wrong to steal rightly just like memory
There so many secret rooms and trees
Of wonder like people
        of recognition of

So many dreams

When I first met Bernadette

(Magnetic Fields sings

I met Ferdinand de Saussure
   On a night like this as I write)

I had encountered the blinding *Midwinter Day* on a shelf in the Brown
bookstore on CD Wright's Long Poem class which I did not take but took
at least 3 others with her

And resolved to meet its author the next summer gave me the opportunity
And when I arrived in the dimly lit room at Boulder Varsity townhouse
    apartment

I brought my copy with me for her to sign and having barely met she
    wrote
I LOVE YOU and her address in the front      I don't remember what
    poems

I brought for her to read but I think one was the one where I tried to
    make a lake
Happen on paper with the letter o like Kathleen Fraser o lake

But then to my confused horror Gregory Corso barged in complaining
    that a kitten
Had used his manuscript box as a litter box but the poems were still
    legible

I am worried since I think I only have 25 minutes with her ever But then
    she
Asks him to read the poems to us and I see one can do that and he does so

With commentary and patter between lines   he critiqued Big Vicki's poem
by saying the MOON you gotta EARN the moon and I always think of
that when I invoke her

If I have adequately honored and asked permission like whenever I pick
An herb or plant I ask permission of that plant spirit or fairy and give
   thanks

Then I realize there is an illusion of charged infinite time ready
Present in the room

We are listening to 69 Love Songs which was the polyamorous courtship
record from my essentially physically monogamous baby daddy husband
I am married to now as the core of my tribe Tony and now that I am
listening to it I realize it's like Shakespeare's sonnet or Bernadette wanting
her Sonnets to be love poems to everyone or at least like Marilyn Hacker's
love sonnets to a girl love so her combo of Phil and me plus others past
present and future loves makes for a wild menu I am trying to write my
version of in real time

We don't know anything about love yet we know it all

And generative. Loss

*My absorption in your clothes is only sensible.*

*You and I are like two transparent wings*
   Elaborating lists of things

*I did put the rest of the clothes away though I did and didn't want to*

Reminds me of my idea to hang all of Emrys's baby clothes in the order of
wearing on the wall of the parlor but that would be traumatic because of
gender

List all the art and Stuff that's on your walls past present future
A partial liftoff art sold for survival
Soldered together to make a wild sauce

Bibliomantic lines Katy's finger chose
Were the ones she forgot to read out loud that afternoon
Predictive like so much of Bernadette's poem is
Like the talk of the atmosphere and having to move to the moon

Be Bear Aware. If you meet a bear do not run. Back away slowly while facing
the bear . . . Alert it to your presence by talking or singing.

Laynie comes for tea and I set the candles on the kitchen island but Rachel
moves us to the living room and says we need plates for the crackers so
Laynie gets them but she gets the cat plates first. Before L comes I brew the
tea we blended for the fires in California, mullein and licorice and mint,
luckily she wants to drink it too, but we have plenty of other selections, a
typical lesbian tea cabinet, just like the scene in *Go Fish*. What I really want
is more coffee. Gina said there will be coffee at the reading also snacks. I'm
trying to write across sound, the stereocilia poem was in couplets but now
there are four-line stanzas like boxes.

I jog; I withdraw cash; I get my hair blown out
The stylist I saw last time doesn't know me
That's ok, I never expect it
Tonight I'll wear a blazer my boyfriend's mother

Picked out for me: herringbone boy school
She lives on Park Ave
And her hair is silver winter sky
I'll never exist in one life
Try as I might

Sometimes, when you take everything off a sandwich,
you make a salad. I was annoyed by poets then, and
"Something inexorable about mothers, a list."

A list of every gift the (in)(season): Diorshow mascara, Dior bright red/light
pink (name of color?) lipstick, Glossier Boy Brow in brown, Avene Micellar
lotion cleanse, Avene thermal spring water, Besame Red lipstick, Jason Wu
for women, Reb'l Fleur by Rihanna, big ice cube tray, small glass dildo
(anal), handcuffs with key/safety//adjacent to Official List of Brattiest
Girls: XXXX XXXXX. Only one name, all caps, like an echolocation.
Shallow and storms. Far more and awakening. I live here, too, in this one
mile radius town. I point to the church, my arms full of wrapped gifts with
bows. I have to go in there, I say to you and we part at the intersection in the
sidewalk, you wild with gerrymander. I'm excluded once more in the way
where it feels all boxing match and TKO.

# AFTERNOON

On our way home from lunch this is a voice memo we see a Mural looks pale blue and gold and white and then we see college hill in providence in the midwinter late afternoon sun the Baptist church spire is white gold some building from Brown is the most beautiful thing we've ever seen Jane says is that real what else did you say Jane about that Jane says it's just like all the other buildings except it's a special building because it's a church up ahead now the state capital the largest the second largest unsupported dome in the world after Saint peters and possibly some other domes don't get excited about your dumb in Madison Wisconsin everyone that no I believe is supported the independent man is on the top he has a little spear I don't know how do we feel about independence at midwinter is it something anyone could possibly value Mr. Scrooge said his least favorite thing the thing he hates more than Christmas remember what it was Jane yeah I I think yeah he said Christmas carols or a Christmas choir and he hates the egg all these people getting together and singing together right why does he hate that James says it was because when he was little he had to be at school on Christmas so that made him hate a Christmas choir maybe and it also reminded me of the guy from The guy from weird team which is the rival adult organization to Odd Squad which is a kid team of scientists and agents will solve math problems and the guy from weird team said he regrets calling it weird team because here comes the police OK the Amtrak police that's crazy I didn't know they had an Amtrak police check police is coming up to the red light and we all had to pull over I'm talking on voice memo on my phone and they're going to the Amtrak station which is a very nice train station but hope everything is OK over there I used to sing somewhere over the rainbow under the dome anyway the guy The guy from weird team regrets calling it a team because he says people should work for themselves and not with other people and that reminded me of Mr. Scrooge not liking a bunch of people getting together and singing they both just want to do things by themselves and I think this is a time of year when we want to do things with other people what do you think Jane thinks you should help other people and work with other people so those are my thoughts right now

Am I Anne Marie
Snow sleepy
With our teeth out
Tell me a murder
and make it mine
Anne Marie doesn't mind

Hugs and hustle and tortillas bitten through
the middle and thrown
on the floor. The children so easy
with each other but also already
breaking down. Baby in the hallway
stealth creeping from the napping
room, cheeks pink. A french press for me
followed quick by a beer.
Quiet for a moment in the hum

of pause and play. We all run
to the window for a deer, city cousins
stunned. She is erect and nervous
at the corner of the lawn
and while we're watching two
babies nudge into view
from behind her.

We go to watch the surfers and look for whales, but there are no whales anymore like there are no bugs anymore and the surfers bob in waves that are, like terraces, flat and wide. It is December 22 and we tally the year's ailments which have been mercifully unserious. Genevieve vows to spend more time writing. I vow to be a bitch at work—that is, to expend less energy being agreeable. Was there a riot at Versailles? It's raining on the horizon. The surfers wait in the zone where the sets come in.

It's time for Vesper's nap, so I coax her slowly, first to pee on the toilet, then to step into a pull-dipe—as she calls them—and then down into the queen-sized bed in the room I slept in through high school. She wants bird sounds on the noise machine, wants her brother's black bear on his pillow, wants me to lie down next to her, wants a song. I sing "My Favorite Things" and mostly remember the words except the last verse, but as always, I don't get there anyway because she has questions when I get to "when I'm feeling sad." She wants to know why sad? And why favorite things? And what will feel better? And why dog bite?

She's sleeping now, so we could go buy more things for the children's Christmas stockings, but mom wants to rest and now dad has gone out to buy hooks to hang ornamental balls on a tree in the yard. Owen is talking to himself in the voices of trains, but we're not sure if he'll leave mom alone or not.

We drive to Fubonn market and walk the aisles and look at canned sardines and coconut sugar and long beans and bitter melon. We get a bag of key limes, some furikake flakes, some gummies, mango and muscat, some chocolate and cookie mushrooms and some chocolate and cookie stumps, two young coconuts that need to be refrigerated and some mango mochi and some chocolate mochi.

At the Wolf House we're still in bed with Bernadette
in the hologram bedhead while the kids
                                      heard and not
pursue each other in distracted chase—crisscross
across the stanzas—the day
sleepy and we are floating in that cloud state
                          the cold mist of melting crystals
oranges and turkish lamps. Are nonsequiturs a form of intimacy? Is ruffled
   syntax
a correlative to a bed after waking—
                             Annette, who has come from a
   funeral,
after singing backup at the Ice House the night before, is a great
if enigmatic host, very attentive to the traffic of friends
and children and people I've never seen. A little boy Louis urgently
   discusses the cockpit

his term for the large round room where the readers, mostly femme
are reading—I meet Nicole from NY but originally MN and Shanai and
    Carla-Elaine and
later Ashleigh and Mary who I haven't seen since we had no bangs.
    Hovering
adjacent to the readers' hips
several feet away and above the entrance downstairs
is a disco ball very still and listening

                                        orb of my love
for being read to when so much of love is so difficult
The walls are trompe l'oeil stones—*What are you doing there?*
one boy shouts from the other room. And the reader at the mic reads
*We're only having spaghetti.*

an afternoon at my desk in the company of emily dickinson, toi derricotte,
gwendolyn brooks, and marilyn chin. dickinson the delightful, dickinson the
delirious, dickinson the terrible, dickinson the inescapable. i pore over page
proofs and pray (well . . . hope very much) that my sense of how some of
her successors succeeded in dealing with the push/pull of her work makes
sense. outside my study window, the "bare, ruined choirs" of our maple tree
—though, indeed, it belongs to itself, or to the "mid-atlantic region" earth
in which it is rooted.

        genealogies—
        what grows where, and why . . . and who
        can lay claim to it

Sky on the skin of the river, portal portal, pulsing tender layer
of ice forms, dissolves, informs. Silas points to a storm drain,
Pennywise lives there, he says. You're right, I say. At the high school
one of the kids says, you look like Shelley Duvall. I do, I say glad
I still have that terrorized-by-Kubrick high-out-of-my-mind look
of youth. Her performance was so underrated, the kid says. Bruno
sells us a cookie and the kids recite the names of the trans dead.
Adam buys some chaga for his mom, and I say text me, baby, but
don't kiss Bruno's head as we leave him there. They've raised
enough money to buy binders for every kid who needs one. We
walk home down the hill where it's just grass and gravel
holding the surface world taut, then mud all the way down.
They sent an email, the sledding hill isn't safe
for sledding. We'll know more later.

4:30pm and darkness rising, over the tops of pine trees whose green holds
steadfast and waiting for winter. Heat of December, small puddles of rain,
five rainbows before night falls permanently. If the trees hold our sorrow,
can we listen closer. Today the darkness seems monstrous and vast beyond
recognition, a knock on the door, the bass from the car comes from the
Earth, too.

*Writer woman poet artist*
*putterer of nonsense*
*player with letters*
*a resolute brick in a broken house*
*a bucket of questions*

What if I gave myself the assignment for the afternoon to look at the past
        and ask of it the truth a list of everyone who was there & all the
        things they said & all the things I think they said but didn't & when
        did I first begin to lose my ears, it's hard to say, because there are so
        many memories that have no sound at all but mixed right up to the
        present with so many obnoxious ones
throwing tantrums in the library of my history & Shawn coughs, we have
        talked about going out to the health food store & nursery or as
        he says the plant place, what of that past? What do you make of
        his opting for those words over the other, the resolute bricks of us
        weatherbeaten each by a big boulder called a parent
Did the house really have a stupid chandelier in the formal dining room
        that no one used except when people came to play Yahtzee, is that
        a real game involving dice, did I dream of the desk next to my bed,
        the papers on it smelling of carbon copies, the tile in the bathroom
        a dumb pink & all the furniture in the living room hopelessly heavy
        as if trying to trick us all into taking it seriously, yes the house was
        yellow & the kitchen was yellow & the kitchen table was yellow & I
        hid under it while he
raged at her & that's enough the hole in the yard I went to sit in like a bird
        *I'm going to put this several boxes down & ask you to type above it because I don't*
        *like always being at the top, it's too much pressure,* I think it's been three or
        four days since I put on any shoes—*I sometimes wear them on Thursdays*
        I told Catie *if I have to go out* but that isn't correct I wore black flats
        yesterday for an hour & went to buy mushrooms for the holiday
        going to the store for food is a good excuse let's get ready we can
        drive along the river & look out take in be surrounded by the day
        the balance tips

★

from brooklyn to a lake woodfire stone burning why does it smell so good and make me feel so nostalgic when im from the city treetops smells like pine 22 jumpstreet let the needles fall to the ground splat nah they dont splat though do they make a sound lights all around they go on some go off i dont know embers

Poets in rows sitting up standing down when I get inside your prose I never trip. I'm deep inside the stripped rhythmic torch we call claws or waves. This is the shortest day and longest night separates us until we meet tomorrow. It's been the most wonderful terrible week because the days shorter seeming longer and the night longer being infinite or slept are all bright sledges of days in which it seems impossible that we've only just met one week ago for the first time.

Podemos ir al cemetario, Farid says.
Ah, si por favor, says Patty.

It's been years since we've been to the mausoleum where the ashes of Farid's mother and aunt rest.

I wonder if Gianna would want to go, should go? Like leaves, I want to tell her as we drive past fallow fields, then a flash of irrigated green in the desert. Closer to Tucson—fields of cotton. If you blur your vision, fix your eyes, they might look like winter branches dusted with snow.

long stretches of green
when the mountains give way
stacks of hay

Yellow flowers on the edge of the interstate 8. Sun on legs through the windshield, sun on sun glasses and the reflection of my eyes. Shadows extending toward the place we left.

Two days from now I will complete another year on the earth or the earth will complete another rotation around the sun with me on it. And where was I before, Gianna asked me once. And where am I now?

Purple flowers on the edge of a highway near California. Bicycles hang from the back of an RV with American flags flapping the breeze. Why does that flag bother me? I think first, then the question reforms itself: When didn't it?

A flock of plastic bags gather on the median, if you blur your eyes they might look like doves. The children speak in gesture and sound. A crow stands on a fence post like an afterthought. 80 more miles on this highway before we can get off.

Be strong and live another way
I haven't yet, for money signals time to build a wall
because exchange demands     I take a side,
and builds a barrier          I could live inside
consuming mortar
until evicted onto sidewalk as a gas
to celebrate your skin

and fetch and carry flying yeast and water
I have things to do today and I will do them as a gas

With hiking sticks she's guiding me
through Conservation Park in Pullman, Washington
pausing when she talks on the narrow trail
it used to be a deer trail, she says
it is muddy, we have boots, it's cold

Plans to pave a road are angering Pamela
who's put footprints down with deer and red fox and cougar
she has a plan to protest, I think Scotty will want to join
and maybe Kayla who is restoring native species to this potential Palouse
    prairie
now full of naturalized grasses, which are grasses, I've learned from Kayla
that, like naturalized citizens, adjust to a new place, and change it, and call
    it home
Pamela's eyes have an angry fire, or is it the wind, will she cry now
for this wild edge of the human world of fragmented prairies

We get to work with our favorite shears
and near the gate by the road she collects thorny red boughs
I untangle the towering hardy stalks of hemlock
a poisonous plant in the Apiaceae family whose relatives include
cumin, carrot, parsnip, chervil, coriander, caraway, anise, fennel and dill
all wonderful aromatic flowery plants
their family sometimes called *carrot* or *parsley* or *celery*
the hollow stalk is jointed like bamboo with notches for easy measure

—where it's curled back Roundup was plied
—it's where redwing blackbirds gather
they look quite smart with red and yellow bars on their wings
they nest only in marshes and just downhill you can see the cattails
shedding fuzz they pull into their nests, imagine
we are all outside our native range unless we are native
settlers here kill things we don't understand
and even think killing is work
an idea Pamela and I flatly reject
gathering pine boughs and rosehips, douglas fir cones, oak leaves and
    lichen and thistle
we resist this dying

She leads us to the Quail Grove she calls it, though she seldom sees Quail
    these days
we drag our stalks to a grassy spot near the ravine
we can hear the water, the sky is overcast and working
we are not too cold, she chooses a bare wormwood plant as the center
it stands about eight inches off the ground, I begin draping it with lichen
it is green and springy and I ask if she would eat it
I would, she says she would if she were very hungry
she arrays pine boughs around the stem
I shred a chunk of bark separating fibers into feathery threads
to bundle and secure in a bow
a drone flies overhead, I've never seen one here
I want to see the surveillance footage

Douglas fir cones are lovely, covered with little twiggy legs
that catch on the branches, she spreads oak leaves
about the base, I lay down a few pine cones on the ground

hang rose hips in one spot, it looks like a heart
array hemlock branches in a kind of crown
we are really getting cold fingers now, we are confiding
to finish the rays around the lower half
and return tomorrow to see how it has changed
already the wind has blown it a little

Sitting on the subway across from a woman wearing snakeskin boots and another wearing a snakeskin turtleneck, and I'm wondering what I did with the snakeskin BCBG dress I bought at the Buffalo Exchange on Haight Street now that I have a black tie event to wear it to. I know what I did—I gave it away in a whirlwind of getting rid of things while I was moving. Matt was probably like, "thank it and let it go." Thank you snakeskin BCBG dress you were hanging in the store window and then you were mine. And the only time I wore you was to Amick's 30th birthday party at the Peacock Lounge which was 1930s themed but who ever talks about the 30s. I didn't look 30s in my snakeskin dress with a perfect sweetheart neck and princess sleeves and Matt didn't either, it was one of our first dates and he wore an Amoeba Records hoodie. I was 25 and he was 24. I had a dumb cigarette holder and vodka tonic on the dance floor. Would you even fit me now, deep into my 30s? I was so dressed up and he was so underdressed and I felt bad but I felt so, so, so, so good. Thank you terror thank you snakeskin dress thank u disillusionment I thought that you would change my life that things were finally changing for me & then I put you out with the trash I'm sorry

The hairdresser says You're not
fat yet, that's good, and then
we walk trading you between us,
worried that the city

                will have demolished
the Middle Eastern restaurant, you say
Look the building has changed

                   but there,
it's just a façade lift. You flash
a toothy smile at the two
people not talking to each other
over late lunch, I feel full

             still
I eat, surprised again by green
inside, and olives, on to another
car a different ring we take
small naps upon arrival thinking
your own crib will lull you quick

                 quick you
cry and want only proximity.

At Fuel the Buttafuoco's not great this time
  or maybe I'm just searching for a feeling
       "coffee93" is the wifi password

               and the feeling
The Riverwest hasn't changed
  in twenty years    I can still get the same
sandwich    the same poets still live here
  paying not that much more in rent

Do you think it's healthy to question
   every decision you've ever made
since leaving     I think it's wise to allow
       that the quest for knowledge
might one day bring me back home


Gripped by holiday grief you drop me off
   at the reading and drive back to sleep
and just as I'm about to feel alone
   I see Austin on the sidewalk
with someone who must be Saidah
   who's come to town to meet his family
so then I'm not alone I'm chattering
   and hearing about suburban grocery
shopping and the oblivious accidental
   rudeness of fathers ("You look like
someone who would know where
   the cheese was") and then I see Chuck
and meet Laura and hear about Jenny's
   Chex Mix family recipe from Texas
via Colorado          It's delicious
   but when she returns with mulled wine
makings she laments that it didn't turn out
   as well as she'd hoped     which is what
her grandmother would've said too
   You inherit the recipe and the feeling
We all laugh because we know


   When it's my fifteen minutes to read I'm
suddenly sweating maybe it's B's breathless

prose or the mulled wine or my sweater dress
or all the words I don't know how to pronounce
    ("amblyopia") but it's perfect because my part
starts with the paragraph about Diane di Prima
    and Gertrude Stein and crazy work for crazy
times I was holding my breath hoping for this

    When I sit back down again to listen
Bernadette has a thought for all my troubles

    "I love to work and pay / The hideous price
of seeking infinite knowledge"    she admits

    "Why live anywhere?"      she points out

scan room still not used
to living upstate always
feeling as though i don't
know who i know
car dependent delay
this café unrecognizable
out of order video
games bathroom too
close walk past reader
microphone to get there
feeling all too visible
dgls says *i don't know*
*who put out the narwhals*

the ability to be comfortable
in company is moving
but i can't stop thinking
of heart rate pulse elevate
i know i need to move
this body more in profile

In my white robe & black rubber spa sandals, I sink into
a too-plush couch & thumb through a book on traditional
Japanese accessories. I love the intricate pillbox necklaces,
& am immediately reminded of Sarah Michelle Gellar's
infamous cocaine necklace in *Cruel Intentions.* The waiting
area is crowded & I move over to make room for others.

I look up from the book & see that M. is sitting down
beside me with her partner. I've met her a couple times at
poetry readings & I love her poems but haven't seen her in
several years. The room is silent, except for the soft groan of
the stairs as women walk up gingerly from the massage
rooms. I debate saying hi to M. & decide against it, telling
myself that I shouldn't interrupt her spa experience with my
approach—although I know full well it's due to my own shyness.
This is something I do constantly at parties or events—avoid
the people in the room I'd like to talk with most, feeling the burden
of my presence. M. gets up to get a glass of water
& I am shocked by how striking she is—six feet tall, a swoop of
yellow hair—then my name is called.

On the massage table, my thoughts wander & I fall into a state
between meditating & dreaming, only lifted from reverie when
Courtney, the therapist, presses hard into a knot at my shoulder blade,
or moves her thumbs along the muscles around my spine. I breathe
long, full & rhythmic through those moments, grateful grateful grateful
for this hour of peace, the attention to my body, the lavender oil
warming my limbs.

+

I sit alone in the sauna—I love the way the wood creaks, a deep
knocking noise, when climbing to the top bench, or when I shift
my weight even slightly. I untie my robe & shimmy it down my
shoulders to feel the warmth on my neck, shoulders, & chest.
After a few minutes, two middle aged—what is middle aged? Am I
middle aged?—two women my mom's age come in, talking to
each other in stage whispers. One has a mug of tea. The other says,
"It's so *HOT* in here" & I had already known she was going to say it.
Two more women from the group come in & loudly wonder
where they should sit. I shrug the robe back on my shoulders & step
down toward the door. "Oh, you don't have to leave, we'll make room!"
one of the women says at full volume. "Oh, it's okay," I say softly, smiling.
"I've been here a while."

**that** afternoon turns to
**the** virtual, a hall of games,
**rhyme** can occur between fear
**of** pleasure and erasure, being sure,

**the** certainty that you will find the
**jewel** if you will pay for it, play for it,
**you** will, oh yes, pay attention,
**pay** the ticket man, pay the villager,
**attention** to the sudden cliff! the bird
**to** your right! will it help you? it
**becomes** your companion on
**your** journey, the mountain top, the
**baby** creature that needs feeding,
**born** each time you fail, hit reset.

I guess it's
Afternoon already
    An inexhaustible poem is being read in rhythms of everyday singing—
    how one day associates
forward and back to past and future plus books and lists and memories
    read at a
     poem podium
of four milk crates full of books

Orange peels all over

Babies around and kids of ours now

Mine texting me      Ordering online food back in the city

    Our writing as a symptom

Laynie writing out of Sekhmet's furry fury

and Bdette's Sekhmet says *My heart rejoices*

Wrecks on the house like

The commas of the *cheapest small onions for the sauce*

Reminds me of a cooking Gertrude Stein combining Alice-like everyday
shopping lists and Gertrude-esque later night trance
tours of Associations. A Fuller O'Hara.

Not to tell them.

Stories.     Made to conform.     P 69

I dreamed of

Much needed

Tongue kissing

I've dreamed that

*I didn't want anybody to tell me what to do*

Getting afternoon sleeps after not being able to sleep last night because of
the bright moon light

A performance of this

Drinking Bloodroot like the garden potion of Rappaccini's daughter

It's the awful solstice

The sun will last 1 minute longer

    A booming other love

*Recover* now rhymes with mother & father

Evening comes earlier than ever before

The family extends

The sweetness is at the wild center

It was only a sentence formed of phrases left by a dream.

Bernadette wrote *David used to say if you could tell the story of exactly what is happening it would be amazing, but I can't do it.*

Then a Whitmanesque catalogue of jobs almost alphabetic then bribery and surgery segues into changes in the sentencing of criminals to the invention of necessary earmuffs

Everything belongs in poetry    drinking ink in the light of traction

Get into my boat with my scribe she wrote
I have great wonder    a lucky pleasure
        Pleasure without any change can be a chore

And

*So just because we're married*
*Don't dismiss us, don't forget to include us*
*In all the gay anthologies as a family*

Song,

For history to be like food
On the table of the window

When I get somewhere in a poem I think that's enough.
That I've earned my keep on the planet for a little longer.
But what would happen if I locked myself up to write with all my might?

All the catalogs in Bernadette's poem. Some are objects, some are feeling surfaces, some move swift and some slow, "There's something about America that's unthinkable." The small sculptures on the wall bob gently when Pattie reads, Rachel laughs and tells Jeff to take a video on his phone. "Californium." "Queer sleep." When it's my turn to read I opt to sit because I don't know I feel fireside chat-y. "I'm not me." I almost wish we weren't taking breaks. To let the light cram in. This would be a good floor for yoga. The coffee served in boxes still warm and Christy's salted rice krispy squares. There's an extra room in this poem.

How did I become likable
And why am I sure it's a flaw

It's not afternoon but night
And my hair looks like a man
Married me and ran for office

There's a smell of a body or of a time of bodies that reminds me of a child
I was a child with in elementary school.

# EVENING

Like Bernadette, I'm trying to read and make soup
at the same time with the clamor of the small children
It's a pleasure to chop red onions and green and red peppers
the same and in between chopping, to read about teaching
fiction and think about truth. I like Nancy Pagh's *Write Moves*, but she says
"genre fiction" is like a brownie mix
                I think any genre, including "literary fiction"
has its formulaic versions and I want students to read Ursula Le Guin,
Octavia Butler, Italo Calvino, Margaret Atwood, N. K. Jemisin,
sure, and Eloisa James or Jacqueline Carey or Dorothy Sayers
and Josephine Tey             I toast cumin seeds and grind them to powder
in the suribachi
Owen says the smell is "intense"        I mix the cumin
into sour cream with salt and put it in the fridge for later
Vesper is whiny and Owen keeps hurling his body
on the kitchen floor and almost tripping me
says it's because the floor is "slippery,"
so I offer to read them some stories.

First we read *Too Many Mittens*, which is a story about how some twins named
Ned and Donny lose one red mitten and then have all the neighbors and
delivery people bring them endless other dropped red mittens until they
finally hang up all the mittens on a line in their backyard for others to come
and claim. Is there a conflict? Not really. Sometimes children don't care

if nothing happens in a story. They like the thought of having too many mittens, of everyone thinking every red mitten they find belongs to you.

Then we read another old book called *Broderick* about a mouse who learns to surf. It's an old book, so I think it'll be good. But it's not. The mouse is ambitious and learns to surf using a tongue depressor that he waxes with a bit of candle. He becomes famous, which seems to prove everyone who doubted him wrong. And that's about it. He retires to a handsome cottage and signs autographs.

Finally, we read *A Friend for Mousekin*. Last night we read *Mousekin's Golden House*, where a mouse finds a jack-o'-lantern and makes a home for himself in it, a little golden room all full of feathers, and then winter comes and the jack-o'-lantern sags with cold and closes its eyes and mouth, so you can imagine the mouse very cozy. In the friend book, the field mouse is looking for a friend, but he keeps mistaking birds and plants for potential mouse friends and then getting disappointed. Of course he finds another mouse in the end when they both flee the same weasel and leap into an abandoned nest together.

I read between the two children. They're always on my body when I'm home.

Is it evening how early is too early the sky's so moody today
across the border into Pennsylvania the light coming in
its incredible angle across the fence separating field from road
& field from field the houses aglow in it
                              I can't help but think
of it every time I cross how I travel unimpeded as though the blood-

brain barrier membranes permit me to inoculate the day with whatever
junk I want & it isn't a lot a useless feeling to notice & to not know
what to do but lament & send someone better another dollar
                                        The truth, says the past
is that all of it happened & for many women & girls & people continues
to happen & happen & the chandelier in the dining room is stupid
& the table is yellow & the truth is a tyrant both halves playing
Yahtzee dicing with the lives of the havenots & we here
                                        have this lot:
to tell about what we see & make it ring for those ears we can
even when we're terrible on the phone & afraid afraid afraid
he's still standing in that room or he's still beating at the door
or he's still got me by my wrists in the aisle stacked high
with toys the year I changed my name at school
& learned to swim in fields the grasses as my voice
it never worked the same again See why I don't write
this kind of poem it's too much skin my dress too thin
in the leak light
                    How early it's dark just a backlit blue
stripe above the hill opposite now the moon not to the window
yet I like how she crosses over the house to reach me    how early
is too early to call it evening, to start some dinner
in the biggest pot to turn down the lights to reach for the
glass of wine I'm being handed
                                without thinking *now* & now is
one of the longest darkest parts of another long dark year & we
will somehow most of us get through it thank you moon a full-on
beauty a cruelty a beauty a cruelty teetering full
& fulcrumming

In my dream my colleague said she had to admit
she still didn't know my name. When Bruno was little
he'd dream a boy had a bug on his foot and was dragging
his foot through the hospital. He wore a hat to bed
so he couldn't hear the bug buzzing. It gets dark at 3:30
and I'd be glad to call it evening. But no one does.
I try to understand a yule log. An original yule log, did it
burn in the great hall for a very long time? I picture fueling
several tidy fires around the exterior of a massive trunk.
I think about how we still listen to Talking Heads dance music.
The kids read an Afrofuturist middle-grade graphic novel.
Adam and I take turns reading Alissa's novel. We talk about
the Christmas tree farm they're trying to sell one town
over. The four of us eat three different dinners. I think about
the marzipan kissing pigs we saw earlier in town. The long
evening stretches its long arm across my eyes. Shush, I say,
there's work to do. Shushshush. The television goes on, everyone
earned it.

reindeers are lit and so are we have sweets? lighters spark joints are passed
they have been joints joints have passed there have been multiple days no
more goddamn look at this floor paid a lot of money for this floor

after late lunch (real lunch) (rocket pizza hummus goat cheese dates around
the corner from the theater), picking up the babies, winter light putting us

through our paces, imperceptibly lapis, we leave the children (my daughters my niece) in a closed room with my brother ("Baby Jail, population 4!"). Paul and Alison and I do a Pokémon raid at St Pius, the air is clear and sharp on our faces, it's so hard to even get outside in the winter with this family. Then I get to go to CVS by myself in the car and that's always the sharpest freedom, putting the car in reverse, more Sister Winter, Jupiter Winter, Christmas in July, the little domestic light displays floating by in the dark. My mom used to say it was the one time of year people weren't afraid to be creative. I feel tenderness for my mother because she hasn't yet accused me of always saying everything is her fault. (This was because she thought she threw away Jane's lost tooth, everyone lost this tooth, Jane's first.) Is it possible to record the bitter impossibility of Jane's bedtime, my mother yelling at me, Alice sitting on the floor gumming a snow pea, every step has to be taken while carrying a wailing baby and chasing a five year old. And amid this the tooth, different shades of white, gray, already dying, its film of blood. I remember that ache and that sharp snap so well, the metallic taste, Jane wants it to stop. Finally she's exhausted and puts herself down on a couch and the three of us are there by the glow of the electric Christmas candle, my favorite light in the world, light of the world, the dark-on-dark horizon behind it the focus of my kid wonder / teen dreams, Sweet Baby James/ne, Silent Night. Now there is nowhere to nurse the baby—don't want to be contaminated by Paul's germ-bed until we get new clean sheets at least, can't contaminate the other beds, all occupied now—so I'm sitting cross-legged on the rug in the hall with the baby across my lap, breathing in fumes from Clorox spray, nursing and thumb typing

The dark night lasts longer in reflected light through windows returning to an empty house unlit and ever waiting a culprit of waiting for one night to exit another until the next day turns into night and I can see you again

between one country and another planet or understanding of time as place. When evening turns out the magnificent glow from the sky we go somewhere. We leave the house or we return. I walked down dark streets exiting the halo of dayglow poets sitting in chairs reciting words which never stopped. When I entered it was afternoon and when I exited it was evening and we were all changed by your hypothesis of love.

Is Bernadette Mayer a lesbian?
Is she friends with our friend?
Do we like her poetry?
Who is that queer
white female poet
whose name starts with—
who my father read
on the toilet
before he left
whose name starts with—
     *I'll show you white lesbian poet*

is it the smell of the bread pudding itself or the whiskey sauce that is the olfactory equivalent of warmth? downstairs, my partner bakes while i make knowledge and art. verbs as the encapsulating (looks like a verb, acts like a noun) of our respective pleasures on this midwinter day. he loves his -aking as much as i love mine. and we each go on from there.

Turn onto the potholes on Mad Anthony
Invisible percussion, he's a general
Who defeated the Miami-Shawnee coalition
To blanchify the Northwest Territory
Where I and others squat
Sometimes to shit and generally in
The wake of war
My genome has arrived, I am .04% Siberian
When humans know we're hybrid plan and beast
We'll change our plans, my calendar gets taller
Coming soon, new project, send your bios
Up behind full moon
Hold it like steering wheel
Not paying attention to the road
The climate stood on end

Hand-pumping a new toddler air mattress, travel crib broken, real pump somewhere on the attic floor. Too many mistakes. Home and back and store and back and home. The afternoon always already dark. Even darker now. What is evening? Is this restful? Want to be reading. Gut punch realization, the typing of others marking this day. Making a day.

Playing Queen with her two older cousins: Take him away, please. You will stay in a closet of spiders for five days. Including venomous spiders. You will stay in a fireplace for twenty days. I'm still holding you very tightly. I will strike a match. I blew it out. You shall eat mercury. It makes you sick, it makes you sleepwalk at night. But what is plasma tv?

You singing I'm dreaming of a White Christmas, then whistling, vibrato, not hitting the high notes, rinsing something in the sink. I go upstairs to wake the cats, you sing, ask if we should decorate the tree. I can't tell what you're singing, you ask how I like that version. I, too, wonder what is evening, it is part hungering for reading, it is prioritizing hungers and letting go before day's end.

Singing again, hungry again, seeking after being loved
I want to sit with him, close, we stop being monsters
fix anasazi beans, spaghetti squash, cilantro
there is much color to absorb in the world
the human eye sees more shades of green than any other color
many think this is due to the prevalence of photosynthesis
on this planet that we call ours but that in no way belongs to us
when you search *human vision color emotion*
you get an article about the psychology of branding
fuck us and what we think of our late capitalist minds
the world doesn't belong to us we don't deserve it
I don't, I try and I don't, I believe we must act on our love
the word *human* has its origin in the Latin for *humble*
if we want it to say us, if we want to be an us at all, live among
freely breathing

Alone in the darkness I am waiting for you to arrive, and when you do you are holding gifts in your hands like fruits. Each one shiny and bigger than the last. There is a sense of dishonesty here in the darkness. One shadow portions another and another and I have been waiting for you, seemingly, all season. Turn on light, lamp click three times. I can see your face now, and I missed it so much. "Here," you say and hand me the heaviest package, tinsel and glimmer. I won't open it. My plan is to throw it away as soon as you leave. When will you leave? Unfathomable that you will ever leave now that you are here again. Winter rain. Sweet sun gone. Five pine trees down an electricity wire. Our lights blink with messages. Will we lose power? What will we do in the silence and dark? At the very least, it is warm. Your hand guiding my hand, saying, "Isn't this what you always wanted?" No. Yes? I'm unsure.

As we pass Desert Park the sun starts to slip down the back of the
    mountains. The windmills still.
The song I don't want to hear says "We ain't never getting older" over and
    over again.
How gold the summit! The house on the hill half constructed rises into
    ruin (Smithson).
What wakes in the mountains? What is hungry? In the backseat, Gianna
    and Ariane
are bored to the point of sleep at 4055 feet above the sea.

All the singers we love are dead. Yet they still sing for us. We wonder if we see ocean but when we see it throws no reflection, we decide it is fog. Beyond the golden bottom clouds, the horizon smears into sky as if drawn with pastels.

Christmas lights hang from the roofs of mobile homes off the highway near El Cajon. What song do they sing under their artificial light? The moon rises in Cancer and the kids are restless, I give them Candy Canes. They ask for audio books. The sky seethes over the used car lot. The moon looks further away. Hung between clouds. Now we turn north, something I have tried to avoid for most of my life.

Ribbons of headlights and tail lights in red and white: a bow of traffic . . . and couples are fighting in cars all over the country (CD Wright). It's a long road. I write in the dark. We tie ourselves together in care and misunderstanding. The moon keeps pace. I see the night's first star as we pass the exit for Camp Pendleton.

Sitting at the bar in Benny's Burritos, the bartender asks to see my sister's ID. I tell him she's 18, and I'm 14. Most of the time I feel like myself. But sometimes I feel like I'm just the goth version of my older sister. She's on the phone with Debbie while I write this. Debbie says hi. We have a plate of so many chips and three dips, one of the chips set up to barricade the guacamole. She has a margarita and I have a glass of sangria. They're playing the Lauryn Hill album, like it's your blue Toyota Tercel in 1999.

I hit another valley so you take over, predictable, noodles and sauce and screeching mouth. I peel four clementines and you chew them, splat them over the edge and onto the floor; we decide on early bedtime. I read and rearrange, rearrange and read, prepping and holiday-less yet in the books we know what's next, mouse or brush or exercise, and this can be ritual until we fly across the world to see you, our outsized emotions still in motion.

★

I want to see Jenny and Laura's house even though, or probably because, I know what it will do to me. All those built-in cabinets and old wood floors, plus attic cubbies and the back balcony. They do what I'd expected they'd do.

At the brewery first it's me and Laura and Jenny, and then bestie Jenny arrives and we talk about murderous men in restaurant kitchens and then Austin and Saidah meet back up and Jenny and Laura leave—they haven't had a day off since Thanksgiving and want to sleep forever—and then bestie Jenny's husband and his friend arrive, and finally you drive through your grief and step through the door.

A rotating bill of readers a rotating cast of tablemates and all night the stars turn in the firmament though we can't see the full moon in Cancer in cloudy Milwaukee.

"We're thinking about moving to Cleveland," you say, apropos of nothing, after a little lull. It's not true, but it's enough to spark more conversation full of fuzzy impressions.

Stormy Daniels is the story of the evening. Not a news story, but the way she was doing laundry at Austin's house in DC this fall. She was dating his roommate and "was on a tour of some sort," Jenny's husband's friend supplies, acting as if he doesn't know the details. We wonder aloud what Stormy's art form is: pole dancing or striptease or burlesque? We admit that we don't know the difference. "So, did you see her underwear?" I ask, and Austin says yes and begins to talk about her show—"No, I mean in your washing machine"—and he says yes again.

"Why didn't you *tell* me?" I say, amazed.

"Some stories you save for Christmas."

★

the last time i had the surgery
i saw akilah to practice for a memorial
for kari i remember akilah said my voice
changed i still don't hear it wonder
if it will change again in january
who will hear the change this time

midwinter day is full of stories
women & dogs notice the dogs
if i continue to fill my house
with books perhaps i'll become
healthy again
                    my dog is lola
is this an epic of the daily?

once upon a time there was a petite schnoodle whose strength far exceeded
her 10lb. frame. she could jump high enough to mount even the tallest
mattress. her bark epic, anechoic. mysterious things happen when she is
alone. perhaps evidence of mice—she knows she's a princess. only pretends
to be afraid.

★

OTW and by the time I return C is practically falling asleep into her
    pizza & B

in an elision of time is full of stories of Anne Boleyn riding headless horses and

carrying her own head in her arms (I picture it tucked like a fucked football only precious),

What *did* Bernadette mean by her lesbian pencil? (or was it a pen/ pen is perm/pen is penis)

In what ways is *Midwinter Day* queer? That its demarcations

go way past a poetics upholding a thin-lipped heteronormative wifery? Am I

talking to me? Who *you* looking at? (Is it Lewis she later/elsewhere

calls arrogant/a pen/a pain to be with?)

&/or like Lise Haller Baggesen's

suggestion

Mother is an/other gender,

when the pigeonholes appear

so

undersized and overcrowded?

The other night it occurred to me: divorce

Stasis and what remains?    Impermanence? Equanimity? When Nada

came to visit last summer she said *your house is like living inside a collage* and for sure there is

disjunction and a hapless affection for horror vacui against the winter which is a desert—but is it

a fixity too? A pen? A sty? What gets walled out? Now I feel an urgency to keep moving

things around. I want to tell you more but it's time to read to B about basilisks.

So just laced with northern light, fried as in
food from the nest we needed after all that

Gorgeous review of ever new and She was
There among us laughing and listening all
Terrible as in beautiful greatness yet totally on
Down to earth roundabouts which range from
Pulling in the bibliomancy—you
Read well—riding the rhythm a heady
Cloud of generative influence going
to the Airport of our mind's eye now
How does that happen? A round house
With a live roof—chewing the fat of a
Full moon—asunder—how much can we
Shake after torn pages flutter up river?

We are going to meet Matt & Natalie for a drink. I don't want alcohol—
I want a liter of water & to stay quiet as long as possible. But when in Rome.
Driving through Sugar House, E. remarks on how much has changed since
he & his friends lived there. The bar is called The Ruin & besides a couple
older men on barstools, we are the only patrons. We sit in leather armchairs
& I drink a Big Brother Bourbon—bourbon, cognac, dry curaçao, cold brew
coffee, bitters, Maple, & a burnt orange peel. The cognac gave me pause, but
it is admittedly delicious. E. orders a Zombie because it comes in a tiki mug,
which is often his MO in cocktail bars.

We follow M. & N. to Millcreek to walk through the bare bones of
their newly framed house. A machine is piping insulation through giant tubes,
filling the clear plastic wall covers from floor to ceiling, as though the house
is made of piles of cotton candy or pink feathers.
The upstairs room has an oversized picture window where we watch

the sun set over the valley. Walking to the car, the temperature has dropped alarmingly; up on the mountain, we watch a dozen caribou run. It is getting dark & I miss my daughter. Time to head back up the canyon.

In the stereocilia poem I keep writing about the other parts in Patrick's ear poem and the metaphors he attached to other parts: the "grief wings" of the otoconia, the "floating hours" of the semicircular canals. I keep writing about the parts in *Frankenstein*. I keep writing about the logic in grammar. Walking home from the reading I see they're tearing up the sidewalk again. What work does a catalog do, one thing is ground you during times of shock or trauma. Name five things in this room, move your eye from thing to thing to thing.

It's been night all day
But now I'm sitting at a table with twelve people
So one of them must be hellbent on betraying me
Just kidding
No one can hear me at a table this big
I love when opulence makes me quiet
To the point of stone servility
Like this bust—an imitation of Achilles
I rarely ever think of food as more than
A task or an event or a country
Because I'm a binary: queen and pea

S. asks if I want a baby, I tell her sometimes yes completely and sometimes no completely. We sit in a silence that opens inside of the sounds of other people, like when in time eventualities branch. I overhear a complaint from C. that sounds academic, and I wonder how we ever do this thing we do. The bouncing knees of my perpendicular neighbor jack up my internal rhythm, the reader's voice crosses both the air and the wires, ostentatiously feminine. I see Bernadette's head bounce when she responds to her own writing with small bursts of sound, and the feeling of a soundless giggle trickles through me. It is the point in *Evening* wherein she names the colors of certain names. I want to ask her what she meant when she wrote, "I am a little bit darker." I learn again, but feel more that this book holds so many of my dearest ideas as dreams, like a kind of writing, like "having it all at once is performing a magical service for survival by the use of the mind like memory."

I sit at my desk dreaming of zigzag ridges on melons
a tradition that I know only in pictures
& watch an album my father shares of himself
with the pictures I can't always read

my father's tenderness
my father's solstice

our small meal becomes a potluck offering
couscous, mixed nuts, chickpeas, olive oil
an assembly of things long waiting to be eaten

In the Netherlands,
early evening is *borreltijd.*

I'm not now in the Netherlands,
it's late evening, not early,
and I don't often drink beer,
but here I'm raising a Heineken
to *borrel* with Bernadette.

# NIGHT

brooklyn might be done but i see it right in front of me sipping on this
coquito

Garlic moon
Winter bread
Fairy brick
Brick landing
Snow safe
Mud room

The moon's a rumor, the rumor is bad, & night has arrived
There's no reason to think of summing this up      the sumptuous
hole of lightlessness that is winter, we always fall into it      presumptuously
believing by March we'll have worked ourselves out like a buried bulb,
a worm in wet soil a green-ass rumor of Everything Is OK
What are we writing friends, to whom are we speaking, each other
I do talk to you here or not known or not living or not him or not
zero or naught free or caught I talk to you & half asleep
with the capsule on my tongue & the glass of thirst he brought me
on the nighttable & full cold moon the moon's full cold
at the window now I can see Laynie typing next to me & feel

we are in a room      I am not in the room with you I am never
in the rumor the moon says go to sleep      I do as I'm told
I speak in the buried tongue a bulb will bloom      sometime

I can almost see your face in my mind's eye but not close enough so as to be
close enough sky. A sky lids face. The wind was blowing mad alone in dark
windows marked out in crayon buzzing as I pulled up to the dark house. I
thought I'd left those dark streets behind, as in exiting, leaving the company
of, unzipped, walking solo on unwritten streets on the shortest night of the
year. December was inscribed by so many feet. And the wind blew until I
arrived to your words anticipating my own anticipation and our messages
crossed simultaneously each saying we could not wait.

we took the bread pudding to C's house, a birthday
gift, because he hasn't stopped talking about the piece
he had last month at our place. we could only stay
for 2 hours (early flight), not long enough to get a slice
ourselves, but we ate fried tomatoes (red, not green)
with some marvelous dip that i might could recognize
if i cooked, a veggie jambalaya, and red beans & rice.
later, home for the night, our catsitter watched us clean
a whole raft of wine glasses while we talked her ear off.
i told her i was writing a collab poem with 20-something
women (more or less) to honor the 40th anniversary of
mayer's epic poetic day. meanwhile, i've been thinking,
not of '78, but of our time, 10–15 yrs ago, when it seemed
we poets collab'ed endlessly, made anything we dreamed.

~~Grace rec~~
~~Thank Daisy~~
Mushroom book
Speakers for Environmental Humanities
~~Read Wynter~~
Exercise
Proof for Jo
Present Mesa
~~Midwinter Day~~

★

Full circle, back in bed—but not the same bed,
Rory & Alison having claimed that room,
The first phase of Paul's quarantine ended, we're
Husband & wife again, but making room
For the holy spirit

*Holy night* I sang
And *holy holy holy* and tonight
Midwinter night, 2018,
Rocking in her plastic bedside pod
Alice learned to sing

Like real singing, pitch changes, consonants
Like la-las and holy-os
We lay here in wonder hearing her voice—
Voice that had only grunted & grumbled
& lolled its liquids now & then but mostly vowelled

And in its rages *ninged*—
For the first time

Tonight, midwinter night, which is really the 23rd, a very desperate-shopping day, usually a frenzied mailing-the-cards day, but it's Sunday, so there's some space, maybe. Still it's a red and green day, not a polar blue; wreath, not star. We'll go to the mall, maybe, or the newish boutiques in downtown Providence, with names like What Cheer?; we may have to buy new phones. The Clorox bleach spray turned my screen into a borealis, silver lakes and blues, the sky today; Paul's won't charge. We were the tooth fairy. She scrawls a self portrait and thanks on a dollar bill. I was milk and I think music. I'm too tired. I basically accused my brother and his wife of being negligent parents in their hearing; I thought they were downstairs and I, too, refuse to watch my children when someone else is around. So why did I say it

The women poets who wrote everything when the kids were asleep

Balancing the laptop on my knees I feel
The weight of this work &
My eyelids

Swimming out of the past day
Drunkenness of sleep
My poor phone in its bowl of rice

I fell asleep just then
Good night

Old moon, snow moon, oak moon, long night moon, full cold moon.

No one speaks by the time we reach the house. I'm done with you, Farid yells at our daughter. And she's not getting out of the car until she does. Patty says the house smells of cigarettes. And I just want to put my bags in the back bedroom where later I know I will find this time to write this.

"I want a literature that is not made of literature," writes Bhanu Kapil.

While Patty and Farid go out for food, the girls play. Exchanging words and gestures: house, park, look. The doll is dressed and undressed. Gianna needs a rubber band so they can make a leash for the doll's dog. They bowl with Styrofoam cups and tin foil ball. They work on a puzzle. They fall into silence watching a picture come together.

Good news a glittery thread sewn into a black dress
Earring holes forgot how to be earring holes, or rejected it
Looking for the note Dottie wrote on my college poem, "how very
      Bernadette of you"
I find a tupperware once filled with Now & Laters, now filled with pen pal
      letters
In the photo album there's a picture of us looking at the same photo
      album on the floor

the best way to understand a place is to build something there
that doesn't completely destroy it for others

I'm in the shower
rinsing smoke from my hair
rising from ashes
to think of this and these words' rhythms
you are tucked into the newly cleaned palette of mismatched sheets
Elsie bites my fingers, still kittenish
the continued demonstering of winter break
if I could write a poem all day everyday could I?
migrants around the world remain nameless
in transit, jailed, raped, and sold
these are news thoughts not night thoughts
Ishi in her quiet way climbs the stairs in our usual night
where you are long asleep, they begin chasing
we're the imagination in this world, imagination force and power
the shapes we allow ourselves to make
and what we need from them
5 minutes till midnight in Pacific Standard Time

I drive in the rain to the reading
knit straight through it like I used to
when I lived in Brooklyn      knitting smooth
hills now in different colors to use up the scraps
words flow and it grows
dark blues and jade and black and a bright chartreuse
which I used to think was pink not green
now pink is here too
Lines I remember writing about alongside
lines that sound new      She did it anyway

tired and doubting and broke and uncertain
I think I need more time to write in an aimless way
or one that's three floors below the light

Write the children singing to the bear moon

The dreams are just airport dreams, wrong or poorly packed
lost luggage, where's the baby. I've got decadent cake I'm not
allowed to eat even in dreams. Sarah shows up, Sarah from
my whole life, and she reminds us that the chocolate's no good.
The DJ who used to run the Top 40 countdown now runs
a vigilante squad. They've attached the villain's face and torso
to the back of the van and outfitted him a gold and black
Voltron. They're having a philosophical argument. They're hosting
a cooking show. Everyone takes turns frying a button-up sock.
They add a fish eye to the sock's button hole, and ask each other
have you ever fried a fish eye before? I can tell I'm not okay.
A day can contain everything, sure, but our days can't currently
be predicated on routine. We need something exceptional
to happen. Every day until we find ourselves enough repaired,
we require, and so I try to engender, something exceptional. I
couldn't really sit still when the children were little and now
I can't sit still because we don't have much time. Night comes
in and it's not the comfort it once was to know everyone drops off
to sleep while I work. I interject that it was a comfort because other
mothers were awake all night too. But work isn't working. Work strings
one month to the next in haphazard attachment. If the nighttime
is the right time for work and love, I've neither most nights.

Tonight I try to nestle a little of both. I read *Bear*, about a historian
who's given an on-site assignment on a private island far north
in Ontario, in a historic house octagonally shaped, described
so that I can indeed picture each of the octagon's planes. A bear
lives out back in an old log cabin. She must feed him dog food
His fur is matted and she thinks it wrong. Chained like a pet, she
unchains him. The novel produces a great interiority of character,
and yet so little record of the historian's reasoning about the bear.
When she leaves him off the chain, she hardly seems to remember
she's left him off the chain. I would never forget something like this.
In the winter, I like to read about winter places, and in the summer,
I suppose I mostly like to read about winter places. Like the historian,
I hate the feeling of cold on my skin, but I love the winter and sniff its air
with my also animal nose. She hasn't lived her life, she thinks, and I
think, well, I certainly lived a lot of my life. She's falling in love
with the bear, but she doesn't say it. I read in bed for an hour of suspended
calm and then everyone must be commanded to sleep and as I do every night,
I try not to let the children see how distressed I am, this day isn't it either.
This day was not the one that would yield.

When is night, when you
sleep or when I think I should
be sleeping, when the firefly
inside stirs and I sing *stay*, thinking
well that is also a form

                        I know our
dates did not align, my
day your night, a slight

                  thing, I tell
myself, checking the air
before sleep so I know what
you'll breathe in the night.

All the way back home
my mom's a late-night
infomercial selling
the benefits of bone broth
and celery juice.
I ask what came after
Paleo and she says,
"Anthony William,
medical medium"
as if the man's
a stone age.

She's dunking her hand
into a hot wax machine
made by Revlon
sitting on the kitchen counter
like a crock pot.
Once, twice, thrice.
I gasp and recoil.

—What is that.
—It's a heat treatment.
—For what.
—I sprained my finger.

—What happened.
—I fell at work.

She slips her hand first
into a plastic sleeve
then into a blue oven mitt,
waving it around cheerfully,
announcing

—That was harder for you
than it was for me.

Everyone's tweeting about the moon on this the second-longest night of
the year.

but where is the monomyth? if an epic is a cycle, then perhaps the
journey defined by dream. i remember the first time my shrink suggested
i "try jesus"—i looked up from my sunken in seat on the couch to see
wooden crucifixes seemingly everywhere. The first time i read *paradise lost* i
embarrassingly assumed christ was moses at least inwardly. the last dream i
remember revolved around my body on an operating table cold from heart
failure—my childhood murmur grown globe-sized. suppose that's why my
breathing shaky despite lungs clear and equal.

If Medusa wanted to change her look
all *eye altering alters all*—were the first basilisks born
when she decided to go for bangs?

                                             It's hard
trying to get by in the muggle world without disseminating
some—to steal the phrase—*homeopathic doses of evil*
                                (all in the I of the beholder)
as if to help build up our collective tolerance for poison.
When we look it up, the old drawings depict the serpent king
with legs—chimeric love child of the snake that married its enemy weasel?
Chimera of the goddess-survivor head. Tawaret was part hippo part lion part
crocodile—a demon and protector of children and if
I am chimera I am part party dress part crone part Sido part Colette part
ghost part dandy part black hole part fern part mantis part moon jelly
part divine whore part those
I loathe and everyone I adore

On my spouse's 50th birthday, the last year
we would live in Massachusetts, in Cambridge,
I read aloud a passage from *Midwinter Day*
instead of giving a toast.

There were many people I loved at that party,
but many of them I loathed.

For the people I loved, including my husband,
the poem would be read as a gift.
For the people I loathed, many of them,
the poem would be read as poetry.

Do I love you, do I loathe you,
how do you read this midwinter day?

I read:

When I was young and slept with everyone
I wanted to    I always loved them no
Matter what—a brave impossible thing
To do it's true—some folks I just had to
meet without my clothes to really know them
and it was somehow a more immediate
transmission—Fool hearty utopian vision
Now I just listen and try to transcribe
an accumulation of Love like a sine wave
That should grow to a swell by the end of
the poem or book—there's got to be a ground
base throughout or it won't work I dreamed of
Writing a trans mom guide    11 short chapters
Written with a woman doctor who is part of me

Eating a cinematic dinner after the lecture
(write down the dream and you will remember more of it said I think it
     was Sarah
Jane Stoner In the sun by the window
          The owner comes over and Implores
Us (me and Monica Youn who in real life helped me a lot this year and
     who is also a poet mother) to enjoy the sun streaming through the
     window
          While there's still time    as the earth slowly turns

So many dreams
    send me off into such a weird space like riding on the diamond sea
A twenty four hour journey into outer space of mind longer form bleeding
    around the edges in crepuscular night that others gather their dreams
    interspliced together with the day

Again we press play and record at the same moment
    as the illumined disc of the Moon
Floats opposite the Sun
on the farther side of the planet    which years ago today
was seen from the moon    the photo of which was said to change
the ways we think of borders and bombs just as this poem
written together in real time on Midwinter Day and immediately after
changes how we are connected all over
                In our own hyper-tridimensional lives
                    inspired by the great lover mother
            despite and because of putting the children or parents or books to
    bed in different decades as well as folding all we own into pocket-sized
    convolutes
of word world time zones glowing
        looking forward to the Spring yet again

Crammed into the pizzeria with a hundred other families—everyone's
    puffy nylon coats
on the backs of chairs, so that there is no space for anyone to walk through
    the aisles.
The windows are fogged with heat from the pizza ovens. It's too loud for
    good conversation.

"I'd like to know / What kind of person I must be to be a poet." I think: *one with others.*

We pay the check & sprint in freezing cold, against the blackest sky, across the parking lot.

On the way home, A. points out the window: *Oh, it's the ice moon,* she says, *I know that one.*

Brenda says "it's okay to overcrowd bacteria with good bacteria." We discuss the gut biome. Notice she doesn't say "bad bacteria." She does say, sit with a food, consider it a medicine. Jean-Jacques tells us after Midwinter Day we gain two minutes of light a day. It's a nice thing to say in yoga but I think I want it to stay darker these nights and early mornings, I love the quality of air and the way food and coffee taste in the dark quiet, I can really hear it

It's been night for two days
Am I to hope for absolution this year?
Or am I to stay in limbo here in this
prosperity I can't stand
I take a picture of Sarah and Sam
In front of the phone booth I can't
Help it that old whimsy is replaced by new
A feeling that a dead business man will pick up
Marty hands me a glass of bourbon intended
For Sarah his daughter and I misunderstand
We toast to my new job anyway
"Bamontes" I reply to Ben's text
And tomorrow I'll put the Betsy Johnson

Dress Vanessa gave me in the Tiffany blue room
It was the one she wore to Sarah's bat mitzvah
We talk of her mother's upcoming surgery
She says, "her muchacha takes her outside
To smoke, but I won't." One middle class
Venezuelan to one sharecropper Chicana
But I get it all I get it all now

[A feminism, this evening]
Impossible to me love anyhow, and I was okay all day today or at least
    trying but the bully.
I'm not sure of surprises if anything does
yet a mirror.
[The queer awakening] [of never being good enough for]
Five tin cans to my windows, which one is attached to you
[men]
(men are no longer)
I'm taken off the phone bill, there, it's singularly yours, enjoy.
How is your mother, by the way? All of our mothers will be dead
or are dead or might as well be dead. Here is one fruit for your sorrow.
One fruit for your catastrophe. One fruit for the cigarette lines on the
    mouth of your travesty.
(men are not my audience)
Jesus is born this day in Bethlehem (or in a few days?) [who invited him,
    anyway?]
in a manger,
another manager,
who needs it.

★

It's Night in the book, but late afternoon
In the day and the man puts the book in
my head in his mouth and I

                    need that breathing
trick to keep my blood from curdling—but
still again his appreciation of his own sound
each time keeps him from hearing the next
one in time to save us from his better
listening to himself. "I'm past the child-
bearing age," he says. I'm not, not yet.
When S. reads it is just right—her voice
settling in to the sweep of pages, just
right this certain sweep of pages for her.
I think, what if we are all the hijackers
of each other from moment to moment,
women needing less to be women than
to be loved by the caged thing, with the
steering wheel behind our lives, but I've
always had a strange way of dislocating
the love in living.

                At night, the speaker thinks
of gender as she prepares to dream, priming
the problem for sleep-work. A litany of
involvement and discovery claiming
(again) everything for the poet. I go to
my affair with Thoreau last May, but
sticking on his claim that in owning nothing
the poet claims everything. "So much time

has passed," Bernadette says before she
begins to read. "So much to add."

Her cane
is hung on the podium made of stacked plastic
milk crates labeled "Battenkill Valley Creamery,
Salem, NY" which are filled with books.
She reads the list she wrote, looks up
and says, "So many dead people."

I had many things to say in a notebook that disappeared. There was the
upper register of the double bass under the clarinet tone, in an apartment
overlooking all the bridges I still can't name. Sometimes when I tell other
people from my city where in our city I am from they look at me with some
indecision, as though to say: how did you get so far from there? I remember
a friend telling me about where she lives now, near train tracks en route to
the city—how she would come see me the next weekend if she could only
pass her driver's test. & another friend who we took home saying how hard it
is just to get out of the house in these times. I want to remember the bigness
of the moon—if it was the right time of year for that round almost fullness
or if that too was a fiction, like the menorah overseeing traffic as we drove
over the highway & into the tunnel, thirteen days overdue. Which is all to
say: listen to how careless I am with my stars.

# AFTERWORD

I EXPERIENCED IT AS a sort of antifeed. All the intimacy that I'd go to social media hoping to find, only to be turned into a product or otherwise rebuked, was there in the shared documents. When thirty-one other women poets joined me in writing into Google Docs labeled Dreams, Morning, Noontime, Afternoon, Evening, and Night—following the six-part structure of Bernadette Mayer's epic of dailiness, *Midwinter Day*, on its fortieth anniversary, December 22, 2018—I realized that, in proposing the collaboration, I'd been responding to a deprivation. Where were the textures of people's real lives in the infinite scroll that endlessly starves us of a desire for belonging, meanwhile mimicking the appearance of connection?

We typed or copy-pasted alongside each other in the documents, a virtual happening. The point was to be there together, writing; we didn't realize at the time that we'd end up with a book. *Midwinter Constellation* begins with dozens of pages of poet-speakers in bed with lovers, children, pets, devices, books, and coffee. The opening stanza features a "daughter / now wiggling out," the image of an actual poet's actual daughter, but also an apt metaphor for our collective emerging as Mayer's self-appointed heirs. She is ever present in our constellation as we reenact her methods, often in direct dialogue with our foremother. (The word "Bernadette" appears in the book twenty-five times, as in: "There is much I don't remember but there is much not worth remembering and there is what I will remember today remembering as Bernadette remembers.") Thanks to Mayer, we know how to make a book by telling dreams, writing in bed, detailing bodily aches and longings, using proper nouns, describing qualities of light, walking into town, shopping, making meals, and remembering while living while writing. The details of our days, too, appear in prose paragraphs, catalogues, lyric bursts, or whatever form the moment requires.

As in *Midwinter Day*, there is the seamless incorporation of the political; any day has its politics, and on December 22, 2018, a government shutdown was looming. Throughout, that shutdown sits in tension with the opening up of the private lives and feelings of the collective. There's room for all of it in the Everything Poem, which hungers for a shared capaciousness and for insight into the farthest reaches of the mundane: "But I wanted to see further," Mayer writes on the second page of her book, and we're her telescopes into the future lives of women, where so much has changed and so much hasn't.

Mayer's presence is felt, first of all, as we structure our days-in-poetry around her model. And then, somewhat miraculously, Bernadette appears "in the flesh" in the book, too, almost immediately. In the second stanza of the first section, a poet recalls a phone call with Bernadette on the previous day, the 2018 solstice (which fell on the 21st of December that year), and we get another dose of wisdom about the relationship between writing and domestic life—this time, the longer view:

> and I called Bernadette around 8:15pm
> To wish her Happy Solstice and when I told her I had been
> Cleaning cleaning so that someday I could finally write a poem
> And she says she does not clean anymore—it just makes things
>    more cluttered
>       Which I now believe is true

A few sections later, Bernadette appears again at the marathon reading of *Midwinter Day* in Albany, NY. As the book opens, some of the collaborators are taking bus and car rides to the reading, and eventually we find

Mayer at the Hudson River Coffee House on Quail Street, just forty-two miles northwest of Lenox, MA, where she wrote Midwinter Day in 1978. Some of the book's cast of characters are there, too—Mayer's daughters Sophia and Marie—plus her daughter-in-law and grandchildren. The daughters keep wriggling out.

Elsewhere in *Midwinter Constellation*, various collaborators meet up in Milwaukee and Philadelphia for additional marathon readings. The readings were the public-facing part of the global anniversary party I dreamed up so that Midwinter Day might become a literary holiday like Bloomsday. (*Midwinter* calls back to one of its own models, Joyce's Ulysses, by beginning with the same word: "Stately.") Also on December 22, 2018, events marking the anniversary took place in thirteen US cities, and in Toronto, London, Glasgow, and Malmö, Sweden.

The wisdom of Mayer choosing the winter solstice as the day for her project is revealed throughout our homage: it's not only the shortest day of the year, but also one with an appealing mix of ordinariness and specialness. *Is this the daily or a holiday?* I find myself wondering as I reread our book. The answer is that here, again, is the epic everyday: it's the day after the solstice, the Saturday before Christmas, and there's a full moon in Cancer. (The word "moon" appears forty times in this book, belying the wisdom shared by one collaborator via Gregory Corso: "the MOON you gotta EARN the moon.") Gifts, treats, and sensory pleasures abound. In 1978, Bernadette's longtime collaborator Clark Coolidge arrives at her house with a bushel of apples; in 2018, my cowriter Jenny Gropp returns to Woodland Pattern Book Center with mulled wine. Reading *Midwinter Constellation*, I get the delightful, dreamlike feeling of going home for the holidays and finding all the poets there, in the bedrooms of an ancestral home.

Part of my hope for using Google Docs was that seeing each other typing in real time might create a true sense of togetherness. I also wanted to use twenty-first-century technologies to aid our performative feat, as Mayer used a tape recorder and camera in 1978. One poet is able to write while mothering because she's speaking her poem into a voice memo; another collaborates by borrowing the use of ampersands from a poet writing just above her in the shared document. Adjacency edges toward synchronicity at certain points, as when one passage begins, "I say I'm scared of getting close to people, getting hurt," and then the next opens: "Weird how you're supposed to be okay on your own." Elsewhere, a poet asks: "In the waking, who is there? Am I alone?" She is and isn't, in the digital simultaneity of our textual lives rubbing up against each other.

Why did I propose this collaboration? I suppose I wanted to find out all over again whether, and how, "the day like the dream has everything in it." I wanted to understand more fully—not by analyzing, but by reenacting—the magic of *Midwinter Day*. I wanted to borrow some of the book's power and reinfuse it into the social life of poetry. I wanted to know how everyone was living.

What I didn't expect was that we would create a dreamscape of our intertwined lives. Even though I participated in it—writing in the Docs and driving to Milwaukee for the Woodland Pattern reading—the book now reads to me like a dream. It begins with actual dreams, yes, but the scenes of meeting up at marathon readings feel just as otherworldly somehow, as if this is what poets secretly do every night, or at least on the solstice as the sun goes down: we go out and find each other.

The utopian dream of the internet, now infested with bots and data-miners, must have looked something like what we did on December 22, 2018: interconnection as oneness, hive mind as oversoul. I'm writing this in the fall of 2020, and a midpandemic longing for collective material life is undoubtedly exacerbating the farawayness of this feeling. We're now eight months deep into a historical moment when many have been forced into virtual life, in poetry and elsewhere, if they're privileged enough to be able to avoid the physical world. Here we live, on the internet, to our horror and relief, as we continue to try to invent ways to feed the deprivation.

*Midwinter Constellation* is a record of a collective day-in-the-life and life-in-a-day; a shared document of poetic inheritance constellated via screens and social life around a beloved book; a glimpse of how we tend to our kin at home and in poetry, and a reenactment of the feminist feat of doing both at once that was first unlocked by *Midwinter Day*. It took thirty-two of us to prove again what Mayer already showed: if you heed one day closely enough, you will transcend the illusion that somehow our individual lives are ours alone.

—BECCA KLAVER

# NOTES AND PERMISSIONS

THIS BOOK IS AN HOMAGE to *Midwinter Day* by Bernadette Mayer. Quotations from and references to Mayer's book appear throughout.

Khadijah Queen's contribution was previously published in *Anodyne* (Tin House Books, 2020).

The question "What are all the nouns that you would at present call yourself?" is from *What's Your Idea of a Good Time?: Interviews and Letters, 1977– 1985* by Bill Berkson & Bernadette Mayer (Tuumba Press, 2006).

The lines "The book is not written for you / You don't have to be friends with anyone in it" are from Mairead Case's untitled poem in issue seven of *DREGINALD* magazine (dreginald.com).

The lines "Where fishmen lounge at noon: where the walls / Of Magnus Martyr hold / Inexplicable splendor of Ionian white and gold" are from T. S. Eliot's *The Waste Land*.

The lyrics "I wanna f*ck but I'm brokenhearted, I wanna cry but I like to party" refer to Clean Bandit's song "Solo (Acoustic)."

The lyrics "I met Ferdinand de Saussure / On a night like this" are from the song "The Death of Ferdinand de Saussure" by the Magnetic Fields.

A slightly different version of Becca Klaver's afterword appeared in the *Post45* Bernadette Mayer cluster (post45.org), edited by Kristin Grogan and David B. Hobbs. The cluster also includes an excerpt from the "dreams" section of *Midwinter Constellation* as well as essays by Stephanie Anderson, Hanna Andrews, Julia Bloch, Stefania Heim, Caolan Madden, Bronwen Tate, Elisabeth Workman, and Mia You.

Evie Shockley would like to thank Becca Klaver for the call to community around this project, as well as the family and friends with whom she shared her Midwinter day that year.

Becca Klaver thanks her collaborators for bringing this dream to life. Extra thanks to Shanna for the gorgeous designs, and to Bronwen, Mia, Lee Ann, Elisabeth, Stefania, and Linda for their help with paratexts. Thank you to Diane Goettel, Angela Leroux-Lindsey, and the rest of the team at Black Lawrence Press for putting this book in your hands.